THE SAFE AND RESPONSIBLE TEENAGER 2-IN-1 COMBO PACK

BETTER COMMUNICATION, INTERNET AND CELL PHONE SAFETY FOR TEENS, PLUS BUDGETING AND FINANCE FOR CHILDREN

BUKKY EKINE-OGUNLANA

© **Copyright Bukky Ekine-Ogunlana 2020– All rights reserved.**

The content contained within this book may not be reproduced, duplicated or transmitted without direct written permission from the author or the publisher.

Under no circumstance will any blame or legal responsibility be held against the publisher, or author, for any damages, reparation, or monetary loss due to the information contained within this book. Either directly or indirectly. You are responsible for your own choices, actions and results.

Legal Notice:

This book is copyright protected. This book is only for personal use. You cannot amend, distribute, sell, use, quote or paraphrase any part, or the content within this book, without the consent of the author or publisher.

Disclaimer Notice:

Please note the information contained within this document is for educational and entertainment purpose only. All effort has been executed to present accurate, up to date, and reliable, complete information. No warranties of any kind are declared or implied. Readers acknowledge that the author is not engaging in the rendering of legal, financial, medical or professional advice. The content within this book has been derived from various sources. Please consult a licensed professional before attempting any techniques outlined in this book

By reading this document , the reader agrees that under no circumstances is the author responsible for any losses, direct or indirect, which are incurred as a result of the use of the information contained within this document, Including, but not limited to,—errors, omissions, or inaccuracies.

Published by

TCEC Publishing

TCEC House

14-18 Ada Street, London Fields,

E8 4QU, England, Great Britain.

❀ Created with Vellum

CONTENTS

LIFE STRATEGIES FOR TEENAGERS

Introduction	9
1. Life Strategies For Teenagers	15
2. Teenage Mental Health	26
3. How To Curb Nonchalant Behaviours Among Teens	35
4. Don't Give Up Hope	54
5. Teens And Technology	67
6. Communication	82
7. Building Good Character	96
8. Life Skills That Every Teenager Should Learn	108
Last Word	119
Other Books You'll Love!	125
References	131

FINANCIAL TIPS TO HELP KIDS

Introduction	135
1. Finance For Kids	139
2. Teaching Kids Financial Management	151
3. Learn To Say No	165
4. Money And Kids	171
5. Savings	181
6. Building A spending Plan	187
7. Ways To Teach Kids About Money	193
8. Young Kids And Money	205

9. Financial Tips For Kids	232
10. How To Be Successful Children	240
11. What Your Kids Should Know	248
12. How To Raise Kids Succeesfully	252
13. Introduction To Entrepreneurship	259
Conclusion	267
The Book	269
Other Books You'll Love!	271
References	277

LIFE STRATEGIES FOR TEENAGERS

POSITIVE PARENTING, TIPS AND UNDERSTANDING TEENS FOR BETTER COMMUNICATION AND A HAPPY FAMILY

INTRODUCTION

The teenage years of any child can be difficult to get your head around - for both the parent and the child themselves [1]. The changes to their bodies, thoughts, motivations and emotions are complex, so it's important to make this transition in their lives as easy as possible.

See the transition of your child becoming a teenager like a caterpillar entering the cocoon of adulthood, these are the years where they will gradually develop into young adults. Though it sounds beautiful and a work of mother nature herself, it's not. These years can be hard for even the strongest-willed parents, and trust us, your teens will test you at any given moment.

Yes, they'll reach a point where it'll become the most embarrassing thing in the world to be seen out in public with you -

even if you're on holiday and there's no chance they will see anybody they know. The teenage mind isn't exactly a pragmatic one and very few things remain meaningful to them - with their worlds revolving around friends, teenagers of the opposite sex and achieving independence. Coincidentally, this leaves you, as a parent, sidelined.

In the modern, digital world of today; always keep at your mind that technology is proving to be king. Devices are been prioritised over genuine emotional connections with family members and social status, particularly social media presence will likely mean more to them than doing homework. All the more reason why they need strong, effective, positive parenting. It's going to be a difficult road ahead, and you have many modern technological distractions to compete with but stick with this guide and you'll surely make it out the other side as a better, stronger-willed parent.

As if that wasn't already enough, that wasn't even the punchline. Though technology has developed so far that you have the internet easily accessible at the touch of your smart phone, you still have all the usual teenager problems to deal with - technology just makes them ten times more difficult, is all.

Teenagers will experience many things through the ages of thirteen and nineteen; in these seven teenage years, your child is going to experience everything from first hitting puberty, all the way up to deciding what career path they want to follow, looking at further education options.

The first change you'll probably notice is that your fun-loving, no-holding-back child will begin to transition into a more rounded person, and not necessarily in an entirely positive way. Often alternating between self-doubt to contrasting confidence - and in the modern world of today, there's a strong chance that this will be heavily influenced by 'Sarah' liking your son's selfie on Instagram or 'Georgie' saying your daughter's haircut looks weird. The opinions of their peers, particularly on the open network of Facebook for all their other friends/peers to see, will always impact their behaviour and mood. The teenage years are therefore some of the most fluid of the entire lives - especially now that technology is becoming the king. Sorry mum, your opinion on your daughter's hair won't matter, no matter how many times you attempt to tell her it's gorgeous.

The transitions experienced during their teenage years are not only difficult for the child themselves but are immensely confusing for you, the parent, too. You were so used to looking after them, being attentive and addressing their every need - now you're probably just trying to worm your way into their now very private lives in any way you can - whether it's listening in on their conversations about somebody's stream on TikTok or your son's fanaticism with some gamer on Twitch. They're things you have no idea about, but you'll desperately attempt to be a part of their lives by trying to grasp it. The fact is, your role is changing, so don't fight it.

Much like your child is transitioning from cared-for to independent teen, you're transitioning from teacher to coach. You're needed much less than you once were, and there's absolutely nothing unnatural about that, most teenagers are the same. Trust that the years you spent caring for your child more closely have prepared them for what's to come.

Trust that you've prepared them for every social media battle, every "Sarah's getting an iPhone for Christmas, can I have one?" and every "Louis' parents have Alexa, we don't". Trust that you've taught them what really counts in life, what's right and wrong and trust that they'll follow the right path - not just what they think is cool. Remember, you can only take them so far, your teenager has to do some legwork too.

If they haven't already, instil values, beliefs and principles in them that will last a lifetime. Once applied, they can use them when you're not around - you're probably not around because they don't want you to be, so they need these values to fall back on.

In this book, we'll take a look at various aspects of the transition phase from child to teenager, and even look further into the future at adulthood. Though we would never recommend you intervene too much in your teenager's life (as it can be disruptive to them building a sense of independence) we would recommend that you enforce a strong sense of positive parenting. It's important your child knows who to turn to when they have gaps in their knowledge and it's even more important that they feel they can trust you for the more serious issues.

LIFE STRATEGIES FOR TEENAGERS

In your role as a parent, your role during their teenage years is just as crucial as it's ever been, though it may now seem as though you're not as important as you once were. Though your teenager believes they don't need you at all, you should know that's far from the case. This is simply a phase in their life, they're only human and it's natural. Think back to when you were a teenager, you probably acted in a very similar way, so first hold the judgement!

They may be irritable, they may be unruly, they probably don't believe in things like Santa Claus or the Easter Bunny anymore, but that doesn't mean they're not the child they once were, they're just making a natural transition and deep down, they need your help. They need your help, even if they don't realise it themselves. Don't see your child as somebody that's hard to manage, simply see the opportunities you can give them to grow.

One parent told us the story of when she had overheard her thirteen year old son speaking of masturbation on the phone, it was obviously a very new concept to him and something he had most likely heard about at school - either in sex education lessons or in the playground. She told us that when she had that conversation, she suddenly felt a sense of panic, like she didn't have all the answers she needed to effectively deal with what he had just said on the phone. She believed he lost his innocence in that single mobile phone conversation, when in actual fact he was just a boy transitioning into a young man, developing all the usual habits and interests a teenager would.

Though you will find many well-rounded opinions on how to deal with these kinds of topics on teenagers on the internet, you have chosen the best way forward with our book. In this book, we'll show you that there's really no need to panic, and instead you just need to employ strategies in order to effectively assist your teenager with the transition phase - being the positive parent you're destined to be.

Shedding light on various aspects of being a teenager and how you can motivate and engage with your teenager to help them face and overcome their problems. Whether it's a mean Facebook post, a group chat on Whatsapp that your child wasn't invited to be a part of or not owning the latest, top of the range smart phone. Or you know, one of the conventional teenage problems, like girls.

See, the world we live in today is an ever-changing one, and things that are covered in this guide today may be obsolete by tomorrow, that's just the way things are in the modern, digital world of present. Since the dawn on time, parents have cared for their children in regards to all aspects of life, including welfare and prospects. This will never change - the only difference now is that there's a much bigger platform to observe your teenager on. Your scope for observation needs to be wider, but again, you should not worry yourself on these matters.

Rather than worrying, as that will get you nowhere, focus your attention on how you can best assist your child in becoming the person you want them to become and somebody who can be proud of themselves. Learn to be more understanding, do what you can do to be there for them, and more importantly, take on board the advice presented to you in this book. Find what works for you and your teenager and run with it. In the remainder of this chapter, we're going to look at various methods in motivating your child to ensure their development through their teenage years and puberty in particular, is healthy - even when they're surrounded by digital devices. On the subject of digital devices, is anybody else just about done with ringtones? Everybody put your phones on silent maybe we'll forget we ever had them in the first place!

GETTING INFORMATION

Not so much in the general sense of getting information, but rather your teenager should, if they haven't already, have an education on the emotional and physical changes they're experiencing during their teenage years [2]. Yes, they've probably had conversations in Science and Sex Education lessons, but there's only so much they can hear from 'Mr Bowerman', he's a qualified teacher, he's not a life coach. You need to ensure that your child feels they can turn to you to fill in the gaps of things they may be too embarrassed to ask a teacher about. When/if they do turn to you, you need to handle it in the most informative, sensitive way possible without betraying their trust, and if you ruin things at this point then they simply won't bring these issues to you again.

It's important they have a well-rounded education on these matters, as they need that self-awareness to know that what they're going through is perfectly normal and most certainly natural. It's also an opportunity for you to support your teenager, so you should look to assist in any way you can to maintain a strong bond with your child even when they go through the 'letting-go' phase.

These changes, though challenging, are perfectly normal occurrences for a teenager, and there's no need to go into any further detail with your teenager if they do not feel comfortable with it. As long as they know that, you've done your part. In the modern, digital age of today, you could tell them to research it on their digital devices, providing they use accurate, reliable websites for helpful information. Providing your teenager is safely, sensibly and effectively using the internet, there is no harm in them doing this. The internet is a vast library of information that is constantly being expanded upon, so they should definitely use it if it spares them some embarrassment. That said, encourage them to bring genuine concerns, particularly if it's about their health, straight to you.

One parent recited a time where her daughter had asked her about her breasts developing. She had said that her daughter had concerns they were 'growing' and she had to explain to her daughter that she was simply just ahead of her class on this and the other girls would catch up. Her daughter then went on to say that her and her friends had googled it and that's where she found out about surgically-enhanced breasts. That was an entirely different conversation to be discussed.

We tell that story to show you that although the internet has a lot of useful information, it can also present issues around confidence and inferiority, where young girls may use the internet, see surgically-enhanced breasts and then go on to wonder why a woman has had surgery to make them bigger. This is why safe, monitored use of the internet is important.

Facial hair, pimples, pubic hair, periods and chest hair are all aspects of your child's teenager years that are sure to also come up in conversation at some point, just make sure you handle the situation sensitively and ensure they know it's perfectly normal. You're doing your part without getting involved in unnecessary, potentially-embarrassing detail.

Remember also that these changes may be the topic of at least one or two social media posts - where false/inaccurate information is distributed daily. So, don't be surprised if you need to correct a few statements, with things like "You don't grow pubic hair until you reach high school" appearing from time to time. Digital technologies are known for spreading information that sounds like it could be true but often isn't - so be careful about what your child is reading.

LEARNING FROM COUNSELLORS

Though you're the parent, the primary caregiver, that does not mean you're in this alone. You may not realise it, but you have a much wider support network of friends, family and other professionals involved with your child's development - all available with help and advice.

Remember that teachers, pastors, psychologists, friends, family members are on hand - as they've likely already experienced a lot of what you are experiencing with your teenager now. Turn to them for advice, support, but allow your child to as well. Ensure that your child knows they have a much wider network available to them. Their options aren't just their parents and their friends, there are professionals and other family members/friends they can reach out to as well. Offer that branch early to ensure they feel safe.

YOU MUST LEARN TO BE MORE UNDERSTANDING

Understanding the enormous pressures the teenagers face on a daily basis is one of the solutions to insubordination. As a parent, you should try to find out the problems your teenage children are facing and try to picture yourself in their shoes. Lessen your authoritarian posture to them and genuinely seek to know them.

Build a positive rapport by patiently listening to all the problems they bring up and try to find the answers together. Give them breathing room if they need it, and stop nagging about their clothes, uncompleted homework, unkept hair, cluttered rooms and unmade beds. Instead, model how you think they should act with your actions and speak less in your home. Actions always speak louder than words.

Listen keenly to know their fears and burdens and be a source of encouragement to them. Try to relate with their friends so that you would know where they go to, and what they do there. Don't try to be a "cool parent", because that will put them off. Instead, be kind and considerate to your child and their friends. This will give you the information you will need to know if they'll be safe.

Sometimes your child will fail to live up to your expectations, and that is okay. When that happens, do not make a scene by scolding them intensely. Make certain to find a suitable balance between enforcing your rules and giving your teen the room they need to grow and find out who they are themselves. If your teenager trusts you enough, you can help them with problems they have with their homework or with their personal life. If they don't want to discuss it with you, you have to ask yourself if you were in their shoes, would you want your parents to be involved with the situation? Be frank with your answer so that you can offer relevant solutions to their predicaments. Relax. Take the family out on a picnic once in a while and show your children you would always be there whenever they need a listening ear, guidance or a shoulder to lean or cry on. Play and exercise with them.

Go to the cinemas, ball games, school play and public speaking presentations. Attend their school's awards day. Call them on the telephone every now and then and let them know they could count on you. Be very clear about your family values, habits and attitudes so that they would try to live up to your expectations. Make them realise that you want what is best for them, even if it seems rough sometimes. Let them know that even when they come short of your expectations, you still love them because you know they did their best and you are proud of them despite the poor outcome.

Don't manipulate them. Ensure you are genuine in all your dealings with them, so as not to give the wrong impression and end up driving them further away from you.

PUTTING IT INTO ACTION

Here's a scenario where the above examples on working with your teens could come into play:

Marissa walked into the kitchen after an afternoon at the grocery store. She finds her son, Todd, sitting at the kitchen table. He's already started working on his homework. She puts the groceries down and immediately turns to him to say something. This moment can go in two very different directions with one result leaving the teen both angry and upset.

Which choice do you think will elicit the best reaction for both involved? "Hey honey," his mom states, while Todd continues to write out something on his piece of paper. "Hey," he mutters, not really bothering even to look up to make eye contact. "What are you working on?" she inquired, leaning back against the counter, still focusing her attention on her son. "Math," he replied, again, not bothering to look up after his response. "Do you need any help?" "No," he said. His voice is raised an octave higher at this response. "What do you have after that to study?" she asked. "English," he replied. "Then?" "I don't know," he said. This time he sounds a bit agitated. "Just look at me. You don't need to get hurt with me. I'm only trying to talk to you." "I'm not upset with you, but I'm trying to do my homework." She could hear him speaking in a tightlipped tone. She heaved a sigh and turned towards the groceries. "You better be done by supper," she said.

In the background, she could hear Todd mimicking her words. That's how one interaction could go, but let's see how the same situation could be handled a little bit differently. "Hey honey," his mom replies as she puts the groceries down on the counter. "How's your homework going?" "Fine," Todd says. He continues to look down as he writes information on the piece of paper. "What subject?" she asked. "Math," he answered back. "Do you need any help?" his mom inquires.

"Nope," he answers back. His tone is short but not quite agitated. She notices his demeanour and decides not to pry. "Let me know if you decide to change your mind." She turns back to the groceries and starts putting them away. "Supper will be ready in an hour." For a moment he's quiet before responding. "Thanks, Mom!"

Of the two scenarios, which one got the best response? Which one would you have done? The second scenario had Todd thanking his mother for offering her help and letting him know when supper would be, so in the end, neither one of them would walk away angry. It is completely about how you handle each situation that will ultimately give you a better relationship with your teenager.

2

TEENAGE MENTAL HEALTH

What is Depression? Statistics show that four out of every one hundred teenagers experience some sort of serious depression each year. It's particularly scary when you think about just how vulnerable young people are as it is, without even factoring depression into the mix. Teenage mental health is important, and its key that you're looking out for warning signs [3].

Again, this is likely a much scarier statistic than it once was due to the increase in social media and online activity in teenagers. At one point, social media and use of the internet was confined to the family computer, now however, that is much different. With the inclusion of smart phones in our daily lives and our increased dependency on having a 'likeable' or 'popular' online presence, depression is far more likely to become a societal norm. With peer pressure to own digital devices and maintain an online presence as well as the child not being particularly happy with what they may be witnessing on social media. There are many factors that could make the child feel uneasy.

Most individuals who experience a form of depression can be helped with treatment. The difference between depression and normal sadness is usually related to the strength of the feeling as well as the persistence of the feeling. Individuals who are depressed usually experience these strong feelings for weeks at a time (often times much longer) rather than just for a brief period of time.

Some common symptoms of depression include:

- Feeling sad all the time
- Frequent crying
- Feeling irritable or angry
- Withdrawing from family and friends
- Changes in eating and sleeping patterns
- Feeling worthless or guilty
- Lack of motivation or enthusiasm
- Fatigue - lack of energy
- Poor concentration
- Thoughts of suicide and death
- Feel like nothing good will ever happen
- No longer enjoying things that used to be fun

ADOLESCENT DEPRESSION VERSUS ADULT DEPRESSION:

Adolescent depression can be very different than depression in adults. In teens, it is more common for depression to present itself as irritability or anger.

Depressed teens may be hostile, easily frustrated and may have frequent, angry outbursts. In addition, teenagers experiencing depression may complain of physical ailments such as headaches or stomachaches. Further, teens who are depressed are highly sensitive to criticism due to their already low feelings of self worth. Watch for these signs, but also understand that these symptoms may happen for any reason during this challenging time, and you only need to worry about depression if it occurs for an extended period.

WHAT CAN HAPPEN IF DEPRESSION GOES UNTREATED?

If a teenager's depression goes untreated, any of the following behaviours could occur [4]:

- Problems in school - a drop in grades, poor attendance, or dropping out
- Running away - a cry for help as teens try to escape their feelings

- Substance abuse - teens may apply "self medication" or escape from their feelings
- Low self esteem - teens may have intense feeling of unworthiness
- Eating disorders - often signs of untreated depression
- Internet addiction - an escape from their real life that actually increases isolation.
- Self-injury - is a coping mechanism for teens and an effort to control the pain inside.
- Reckless behavior - engaging in dangerous behaviors because they have stopped caring.
- Violence - more often seen in teenage boys, self hatred is sometimes acted out
- Suicide - any thoughts, comments or behaviours should be taken very seriously. If your teen is talking about, writing about or making suicidal gestures you should seek professional help immediately.

WHAT TO DO IF YOU THINK YOUR TEENAGER IS DEPRESSED:

As is stated in the beginning of this book, depression is usually treatable and is treated through talk therapy, medication or a combination of the two. But you need to first be looking out for the signs, particularly those signs that may have been hidden from you, like social media for example.

If you suspect that your teenager may be depressed, you should try to talk to them about it in a very nurturing and non-judgmental way and let them know you are there to support them. It can be very powerful to validate their feelings and to just listen without trying to educate or lecture them. Hopefully, your teenager will feel a sense of relief that they are able to talk about what they are experiencing, however if they continue to deny that anything is wrong - don't take their word for it, continue to be weary of their feelings and actions and seek help if necessary. It may be too scary or embarrassing for your teen to admit something is really wrong, however, as the parent you know your child and you should trust your instincts. It is best to get a professional opinion if you are truly feeling like something is wrong.

Your teen's primary care doctor is qualified to do a depression screening and to rule out any other medical problems which may be causing the symptoms which they are exhibiting. If there is no medical cause, your doctor can refer you to a health specialist to help your teen through this time. Spoken therapy, or counseling, with a licensed therapist or psychologist can be very helpful in assisting individuals in understanding why they are depressed and in developing strategies for managing depressive feelings. I have worked with many, many teenagers who are able to fully manage their symptoms of depression through prayer and talk therapy. Depending on the circumstances of the depression, there can be noticeable results very quickly for both the teen and for those around them. It is important that teens find a therapist with whom they can connect with and open up to. Trust between them and their therapist is a significant key to successfully getting through depression and allowing the therapy sessions to make as big of an impact as possible. It is completely acceptable and appropriate for teens and parents to screen or interview a potential therapist to determine if the individual will be a good fit.

Rightful thinking is very important for people of all ages, old or young, male or female. The important thing is to remember what you're thinking about and why you're thinking about it. What you're thinking about needs to be the truth, needs to be morally right, lovely, admirable, excellent, something praiseworthy and something that can bring joy to your life.

Take Paul, for example, who was thinking about sports: For Paul, he wanted to be a great basketball player. He practised his layups for hours, dribbled until dawn, and tried to perfect his jump shot. Paul spent hours on the court, all in hopes to be the one that all the scouts were after. The problem was that while he had a passion for the sport, basketball didn't always love him. In many cases, he realised that his drive to be the best basketball player on his team was leaving him disappointed and unhappy. When others were praised for their talents, Paul would feel ashamed. He began to think less of himself and doubted his abilities. No matter how many times he was out there practising, he couldn't seem to find a way to be the very best.

One day, his therapist reminded him of a scripture about mediation. She urged him to try it, explaining that by meditating, he could open himself up to what his inner mind is telling him and that would help him see if being the best basketball player on the team is honestly as important as just enjoying the sport. It's alright to have a love for something, but that passion shouldn't overcome you to the point where you no longer enjoy it, and Paul took her advice. That night, he went home and explained to his parents what his plan was. He shut his bedroom door so he would be alone with his thoughts, and practised meditation the way his therapist taught him. He observed his thoughts, he listened to what was going on in his inner mind, and he breathed so well that the focus was only on what was important. Then, it came to him, just as he had hoped. He decided that all that really mattered was that he was happy, healthy, and still had the joy in his heart for the sport. Everything else paled in comparison to that. The meditation helped him with the feeling of a renewed hope. He also felt more lively than he had in a while. Rightful thinking worked for Paul, and it could work for your teen too. They can meditate on any part of the scriptures in line with whatever they have going on in their life, with this example being a possible starting point.

Sometimes, taking certain antidepressants can be effective in dealing with depression. Antidepressant medication helps the brain in releasing the neurotransmitters that aren't active when someone has clinical depression. Antidepressant medication doesn't always work the same for everyone, and parents should be aware that it will affect teenagers differently than it would with adults. As with all medication, there are risks and side effects present.

With your teenager's consent, consult a doctor about choosing the medication right for your teen. Encouraging exercise and social activity is also very helpful for teens who are experiencing depression. Many teens find art, journaling and drawing in addition to traditional athletics helpful when feeling depressed.

Provide your child with avenues to distract themselves from the complicated feelings they may be feeling. Parents who are dealing with a depressed teen may feel very overwhelmed themselves, which can make this a scary and uncertain time. It is important that parents take care of themselves and tend to their own needs in addition to the needs of their teen. Parents should have their own support during this time if feeling overwhelmed, whether this is the support of a friend or family member, a life coach or their own therapist.

In addition, most parents find it helpful to educate themselves about what depression may feel like and the process their child is going through. This can be done through the internet, talking to a doctor or to their teen's therapist, or through educated readings about depression. It is also important for parents to not blame themselves or each other for their teenager's depression. Depression can be caused by many factors so it is unlikely that any one person or thing has caused the situation. Remember, the good news is that most teens are able to feel better through one of the interventions mentioned above, and learning about depression and it's treatments is the first step towards getting your teen the help they need.

3

HOW TO CURB NONCHALANT BEHAVIOURS AMONG TEENS

Does your teen constantly defy you? Refusing to do what you ask of them? Well, you're not alone. This is probably the sole aspect of parenthood that all parents share when their child is transitioning into a teenager [5] - a young adult who's possible struggling to accept themselves, sees their parents as the enemy and faces peer pressure at every turn. Regardless of the reason your teenager is acting out in this way during the transitional phase, you're likely sick and tired of putting up with their defiant behaviour and you're turning to this book for some answers.

The first thing to remember is that this is not out of the ordinary, every parent experiences it and some teens demonstrate their frustrations in a much stronger way than others. You also need to understand that your teenager may be hiding a lot of tension, particularly feelings, from you. These tensions and changes in their body will inevitably lead to frustration and nonchalant behaviour is naturally going to follow. There are many complexities in your child's development process that make this an unavoidable aspect of parenthood.

That said, it's also entirely possible that your teenager is particularly defiant and takes things to the extreme. It's possible that they consistently refuse to do what you want them to do. No matter what you ask or expect, your teenager defies you. They always resist your authority. Every day is a tug of war between you and your teen, always a struggle for power in the house. Just once, you'd like your teenager to do what you want them to do without questions and attitude.

One parent shared her son's story from when he was a teenager and the parent struggled to cope with his son's transition from childhood to teenager. Much like the teenager was struggling to come to terms with the transition process, his changing emotions and growing body, the parent was at a loss of how to deal with the frustration his son was feeling. From time to time, his son would reveal that he was struggling to cope and was constantly fearing failure academically due to the constant distractions of modern daily life. He said the peer pressure to say 'relevant' and 'active' on social media was becoming too much and causing him to act out. Many of his peers felt as though grades, assessments and exams weren't essential, or at least weren't being seen as particularly important.

As we mentioned earlier, technology has become king, particularly in the playground, and though we may not fully understand exactly what it is about modern technology that creates such a buzz for teenagers, but we do know that digital distractions can cause negative patterns of behaviour. In the anecdote, the father struggling to come to terms with his son's changing behaviour was all a bi-product of the negativity caused through overuse of digital technologies, particularly social media on the son's smart phone. Though technology is good for keeping us in the loop with news, current affairs and much more, it's about time that parents really understood the pitfalls of modern technology in this digital age - and maybe even take a stand against it.

But let's get back to how exactly we can deal with the situation at hand. Your teenager is acting out, he/she is stressed, defying your requests. What do you do? Well, you have a number of options available to you, however, as the parent, it's your job to find the best solution for your unique situation. But remember, you shouldn't force teenagers to do what you want them to, this may only lead to them resenting you, or maybe writing some really dark song about you when they hit the big time in the music business. There are many strategies available to you that you can use to manage defiant behavior. Here are somethings to keep in mind when dealing with your teen who just doesn't seem like they want to listen.

PICK YOUR BATTLES

The first rule of fight club, I mean young vs old club is that you need to learn when to pick your battles [6]. Remember that your teenager is probably raring to go and could easily sink their teeth into a heated argument at the drop of a hat. Quite frankly, teenagers can be savage. When provoked or put on the spot, they will go for the jugular. Be warned and know what you're getting yourself in for if you opt not to follow the advice set out in this subsection. A flurry of emotions has consumed their brain, they're not thinking straight, bear that in mind. This could be for many reasons, as we have discussed.

Whether it's because they're not accepting the way they look, they're worried about failing an exam or assessment or their simply just too focused on their social lives, if your teen is consistently defiant, then they're going to be defiant no matter what. That means that if you don't watch yourself, you could find yourself in constant battles with your teen over every little thing.

Not every battle, however, is worth fighting. If it's cold

outside and your teen really doesn't want to wear a coat, maybe trying to get them to wear a coat isn't worth fighting over. Instead of battling with your teenager on it, let them learn their own lesson by sending them out shivering, they'll soon learn you were right and that they should take on board your advice more often. If you're going to go to war, choose the battles that matter. How do you do this? Before starting a conversation, ask yourself the following questions:

- Is this battle worth fighting?
- Is there a genuine, life-threatening or potentially harmful consequence of what may happen? If not, it may be worth reconsidering

RESPONDING CALMLY AND RESPECTFULLY

Yelling, screaming, nagging and lecturing are just some aspects of parenthood that initially appear normal; in theory, you'd think these aspects would work, but in actual fact, they do nothing [7]. These methods are tried and tested, to be ineffective. Showing disrespect, anger and arguing back only make your teen more defiant.

You may be annoyed that your teen seems to spend their life on social media, or all their spare time on Call of Duty, but that doesn't mean you have a case for a heated argument.

Yes, you should apply effective parenting techniques to guide them into being more productive, but think about what the right and wrong methods to apply in that situation would be.

Rather than opt for a heated argument, as we have advised not to, instead adopt a more calm and respectful approach. Use a more inviting tone to address defiant, unruly or unproductive/negative behaviour and open your teenager's mind to something that would better occupy their time. This is all about finding a more positive way of encouraging your teenager to do something different, away from technology and away from potentially unruly peers at school. Sometimes, it's not about what you say, it's about how you say it. Especially at this point in your child's life, they will likely take everything personally, even your tone of voice, so keep that in mind.

See, some teenagers will actually get a kick out of simply just trying to cause trouble with their parents, especially if your teenager enjoys the spotlight from time to time. Refuse to get hooked on the drama they are so used to seeing on social media and in viral videos. Don't take the bait and maintain a positive, happy mindset. This way, you will have a much better chance of putting a stop to any potential tension that may be building, and more importantly, avoid arguments. Show your teenager the respect any other person in your life would deserve and that way, they'll never get under your skin again.

The fact of the matter is that you should really treat your teenager in the same way you would wish to be treated by them and anybody else around you, regardless of how nonchalant they are. Though it may be difficult at times, particularly if you're competing for their attention with the likes of Instagram filters and Snapchat stories, take the moral high ground. We whole-heartedly believe you can do it, but it's going to be hard. After all, you're in a fight for survival with a teenager growing up in the modern digital age of today where smart phones and social media are commonplace.

Eventually, regardless of the situation or the cause of the conflict between the two of you, your teenager will become tired of trying to argue with somebody who just won't fight back. Your social media addict and your virtual reality recluse all want the same kind of things when you peel back the layers - they're desperately fighting for independence, probably without the skills to actually do it. Let them make a mistake or two from time to time and know to approach every situation with a positive, open mind.

SET AND ENFORCE CONSEQUENCES FOR NONCOMPLIANCE

Before asking anything of your teenager, you must first determine the consequences for noncompliance.

A parent friend of ours once told us that they asked their teenage son to do the dishes. Being a teenager, he wasn't best pleased and chose to act out rather than just get on with the chore that had been asked of him. He acted out, yelled, stormed up to his room and went on his games console. The parent, having not set any particular boundaries or repercussions for noncompliance, he didn't know how to respond to his son's unwilling behaviour. He was puzzled as to how he should react, he told of the questions that spiralled around his head. "Should I have shouted?" he asked.

The situation the parent had found himself in was a biproduct of a failure to prepare for the worst case scenario - but a common scenario. What do you do when your child defies your request? Coming up with a punishment/consequence in the moment can be bad, or can just leave you speechless - meaning your child just gets away with their defiant behaviour altogether. The last thing you want to do is come up with a consequence when you're angry though, so avoid that situation and have a plan in place for when the inevitable situation arrives.

The consequence you settle on should be one that makes an impact but at the same time isn't detrimental to your teenager. You want them to realise the importance of their actions and how defiance in life isn't going to get them far in life, but you need to consider their feelings too. It's a very difficult, very careful balance.

Fortunately, there doesn't have to be a 'consequence' in the traditional sense of the word, sometimes the consequence comes naturally. If your child doesn't want to eat, then they go hungry. If your child doesn't want to do their homework, they face consequences at school from teachers. They may face detention, they may get a verbal warning from a teacher. You can rest easy knowing that your teenager will face a natural punishment.

That said, not all situations have a natural consequence attached to them, meaning you sometimes need to intervene. Deciding not to do the dishes should therefore mean you have a punishment in place to accommodate their decision to not do the dishes. If they make that choice, they must forfeit their time on their games console, tablet, mobile phone and/or social media activity. In today's digital age, this means a lot to them, so you know they will soon give in and just do the dishes next time the scenario plays out.

There may be times when it is unclear whether or not your teenager should face consequences for their actions. For this reason, we have devised a checklist of sorts. A consequence is appropriate when:

1. Defiance doesn't lead to a natural consequence - your intervention is therefore required.
2. Defiance leads to a consequence that isn't significant enough for your teen.
3. Defiance will lead to a situation that puts your teenager at risk of harm.

At the end of the day, your teenager should not be able to evade the consequences of noncompliance.

NEVER TAKE IT PERSONALLY

We know, it's easier said than done. In life, we tend to take any situation that threatens to spoil our happiness in a more personal way. It seems easy to think the world is against you, when in actual fact you've just been dealt a bad hand at that moment in time. It's because of this that people tend to respond in counter-productive ways which result in useless, unproductive power struggles that only serve to make the situation more tense.

If your teen is generally behaving in an unruly manner then their defiant behaviour isn't just a choice at this point, it's likely just a way of life. That said, the important thing to remember is that it's not about you, it's about them. Their defiance is not a result of them disliking you, because that is probably very far from the truth. Your teenager likely defies you and all the other figures of authority in their lives. It's just the way they are and it's perfectly natural for them to act out in this way, but it doesn't mean it should go without punishment.

This segment of the chapter is instead aimed at encouraging you not to take their behaviour personally, because it's not personal. That is just teenagers. Once you accept the way things are now, it gets so much easier, and you quickly learn there are much better ways of responding to their typical teenage behaviour than just scream and get emotional. It's all about being calm and effective.

One parent told of a time where their teenager had their eyes glued to their mobile phone. Social media had become a priority to her daughter and she was taking it personally because she assumed it was because her daughter didn't wish to speak to her mother. In actual fact, teenagers today just love technology and unfortunately fall under the hypnotic spell that social media has on many people. It's simply too hard for them to put their phones down, it's not personal.

PROVIDE CHOICES

As we have already discussed, it's perfectly normal for your teenager to want more independence, even if they aren't really ready for it. Defiant behaviour is therefore often a bi-product of their desperation to gain control and power over their lives and how they wish to live. Nobody, child, teenager or adult wishes to be controlled, there's something built within us that means we're programmed to seek freedom - it's natural.

Of course your teenager doesn't want to be told what to do, who does? Whatever your teenager wants, they will find a way of trying to make it happen, much like we all do in our adult lives. The only thing with a teenager trying to do this is that they aren't equipped with all the necessary tools to execute their plans effectively yet. They're still learning.

Your teenager will never understand this during this point in their lives though, and this is a huge source of conflict in many families. It's for this reason that teenagers are so defiant when it comes to figures of authority in their lives, parent, relative or teacher - whoever it may be. Nobody will stand in their way.

So, it's important to expect some form of resistance from your teenager. Whether it's a refusal to do the dishes or simply not living up to your expectations in a way that really disappoints you, like not getting their expected grades in class.

A way to lessen the resistance you get from your teenager is to allow them a bit more freedom, as scary as that may initially sound. Don't worry, because there is still a structure to follow regarding this. Rather than instructing them to do the dishes, you give them the choice of which chores they wish to do. They must do one/some, so let them decide. Give them the illusion of choice; providing a framework for them that also projects a sense of freedom - and gets them working for their allowance!

Allowing your teen to choose empowers your teen and increases the chances they'll follow through. This is because they own the choice. They're in control because they control the decision.

That said, not everything should be on the table for discussion. Sometimes, your teenager needs to follow the rules and get the job done that is asked of them. Where possible, try to follow this structure. Not only are their benefits for the positive development of your child, but you'll probably see that more jobs are done around the house, and who knows, you may even get to put your feet up and relax for a bit. After all, it's probably time for some kind of role reversal, you probably deserve a break!

PRAISE COMPLIANT BEHAVIOUR

Contrary to what you may believe, teenagers care a lot about what their parents think of them. Defiant teenagers receive much more criticism and almost always face disapproving looks than they do praise and recognition. It's probably justified, but imagine how it makes them feel.

They hear a lot about what they do wrong. Rarely do they hear what they've done right. They hear about their flaws, but not hear about their strengths. Even the most out-of-control teenager wants to be praised from time to time, it's human nature.

Where you believe it to be necessary, you should never be discouraged from giving praise to your teen for complaint behavior. Sometimes they just need a pat on the back for a job well done.

STRENGTHEN YOUR RELATIONSHIP WITH YOUR TEEN

It should go without saying that the stronger your relationship with your teenager, the greater the chances are that they'll positively respond to your guidance and instruction. If your teenager has a certain degree of respect for you then they will likely wish to gain your approval.

Of course, strengthening your relationship with your teenager is much harder than it sounds. As you know by now, teenagers are very complicated to 'manage'. But, if your teenager has respect for you and you share a healthy bond, they are more likely to genuinely care about what you think of them.

If you do have a strong bond with your teenager, don't expect them to be shouting it from the rooftops or posting about their love for you on social media, because it won't happen. Just rest easy knowing that your job as a parent is that bit easier going forward - you're less likely to run into acts of defiance.

USE 'BROKEN RECORD' TECHNIQUE

As we mentioned earlier, you should probably expect a little kickback from your teenager when you ask them to do something. That's why you might need to employ the 'Broken Record' technique. This will help you to avoid the disaster that is the power struggle and the inevitable stress and tension that usually follows.

It works by simply repeating yourself, repeat what you need to say over and over again, much like a broken record would. Regardless of what your teenager says, just carry on repeating yourself, using the exact same words over and over again. Same words, same volume, same tone. Stay calm and follow the technique for the best results. Your teenager will get bored eventually.

One parent once told a story of the time he employed the 'Broken Record' technique and his teenager actually responded by saying "Gosh, you sound like a broken record". He responded with "Yes, that was the plan!". It might be annoying, but they soon give up just to get you to be quiet. Everyone's a winner.

TAKE A TIME OUT

It's okay to call a time out if it means avoiding unnecessary drama, tension and saying the wrong thing. If it means you can avoid a power struggle with your defiant teenager, call a time out so both parties can calm down.

That said, don't leave the situation and allow the issue to die without first reaching a resolution of sorts. Revisit the issue in a calm way after the time out and you can discuss things without the tension that previously built up.

Give your unruly teenager some time to vent to their friends on social media, if that's what they feel like doing, or let them go on a shooting spree on Call of Duty, if they want to do that too. Whatever it is that they need to do to chill out, as long as it is within the realms of the law, allow them the freedom to do it. Only then can you sort your issues.

PUTTING IT INTO ACTION

Thomas was tired of coming home from work to find that his son Mark doesn't do anything from the minute he comes back from school until dinner time. Thomas wished to have a child that will do what his mother told him to do, but she was always complaining that Mark only wanted to play video games and argue with her.

One day, he decided that he was going to change things for the better. The only problem was that Thomas didn't really know how to get that done. He thought it'd be more comfortable, but it turned out he might just have to learn to pick his battles, just like his wife previously had to do.

Thomas walked into the bedroom to see that Mark was sitting on his bed, a controller in his hand and his bedroom in a mess. "Hey, bud. How was school today?"

"Fine!" he responded. Mark continued to play, careful not to get his character killed in the game.

"That's good, but maybe next time you could elaborate more than just fine," His dad smirked as he continued to examine the state of the room. He shook his head, surprised that anyone would want to live that way.

"Your mom says she told you to clean your room". "I will," Mark said, never looking away from the screen.

"How about now?". "When I'm through playing," he replied.

"No…how about now?". "Ahhhh…man." Mark dropped his controller as his character died on the screen. "Look what you made me do. Dad, please get out of my room!".

At this point, Thomas could feel his blood boiling. "This is my house, and I am saying you must clean your room, so you clean your room". "Why do you need to nag? You sound like Mom. I'll do it in a minute." Mark tried to turn the game back on.

Thomas stepped in front of the TV. "No. You'll do it now," he stated, raising his voice a little louder than expected. "You're not being fair," Mark yelled. "It's my room, and if I like it dirty, then I like it dirty." Thomas glared at Mark. "Fine. You can live in your room then. Don't come out until it's clean."

He was mad with his son's defiant behaviour, so he slammed the door closed as he left. Things could have been simpler and not gotten so far out of hand if Thomas handled it a bit differently. A compromise could have been made in the form of a deal. Thomas could have offered that if Mark cleaned his room then he would have played a game with him.

The moral of the story is that it doesn't always hurt to find a compromise - sometimes it means you avoid a lot of unnecessary tension and drama that would usually leave both parties annoyed and frustrated.

Finding a happy medium can be positive and productive for everybody involved, it's important to remember that.

4

DON'T GIVE UP HOPE

In life, you will hear wise proverb after wise proverb, ancient teaching after ancient teaching and just general life advice in bucket loads, if we're being frank. With that said, there's a message we believed you should certainly hear, relating to parenting, highlighting that just because the journey is difficult, it doesn't mean there isn't a rewarding light at the end of the tunnel.

A wise man once said, "We must accept finite disappointment, but never lose infinite hope".

Martha and Conner were certainly trying to follow this quote when it came to their fourteen year old son Tristan. Tristan used to be a sweet, viola-loving primary/middle school student who played on the soccer team. But when he got to high/secondary school, he pulled a complete 180 and dropped out of orchestra and soccer. Though it sounds drastic, this is pretty much commonplace for a teenager today - especially one who may be self-conscious and confused about who they are and what they want to be. Remember, it's a very difficult point in a young person's life.

Martha and Conner were unsure of what to do when their son was going through this transition. At first, it was small things, like doing chores hours after he was first asked to do them. But then his first report card came, and his parents were shocked to find he had C's in all of his classes. When he was younger, Tristan did all of his homework on time. How could he be so close to failing all of his classes? Martha asked him this very question, and was shocked when he told her that he "had more important things to do than homework". What could that mean?

Tristan's laziness started to affect everyone around him. He put off his chores and told his parents he'd do them later, but never finished cleaning. This left cleaning the house to his parents, both of which were already busy with full-time jobs. As he grew irritable and moody, his parents became frustrated. Again, as drastic and out of character as it may sound, was and still is today, commonplace. Conflict with parents due to severe transitions in personality, character and interests is bound to occur, what matters is how these situations are handled.

Neither of Tristan's parents wanted to accept that they were upset, and ended up taking out their frustrations on each other. One night, Martha prayed for a sign of hope that Tristan wasn't doomed to be unruly for the rest of his life. She prayed this every night and was going to give up hope herself when she got a call from a friend. Her friend also had an unruly teen and knew of Martha's situation. The friend told her about a counsellor at a learning centre who helped keep her son on track. But Martha was unsure; nothing she and Conner had tried worked. Would it really be worth it to seek a counsellor?

Many parents choose to go down this route when faced with an unruly teenager who experiences drastic personality changes and acts out because of it. The important thing here is to point out that seeking the help of a counsellor is perfectly natural and normal, there is certainly no shame in it.

Conner thought it was a good idea. They set up an appointment with Leah, the counsellor, and drove Tristan to the learning centre the very next day. When they dropped him off, they were nervous. Leah promised them that she'd be a good source of help. But they had yet to see her work in action. When they picked up Tristan from the learning centre, they discovered that all of his homework was done! Nothing changes, if nothing changes, right?

Leah had sat him down and worked through all the problems, one by one until he caved and did the work. This was great news! Martha and Conner were excited for their new, more positive son. There was one problem, however: when they got home, instead of doing his chores, Tristan went into his room to play video games. They may have gotten him to do his homework, but he still refused to do anything else. Some behaviours appeared to be sticking around for the long haul.

Martha called Leah and asked what went wrong. "I had to work really hard to get him to even start," Leah explained. "Tristan didn't do his work until I broke down each problem for him individually. He's a smart kid, but he just doesn't want to do anything!" Martha sighed. This was frustrating news. She and Leah decided that he should continue going to the learning centre, and Martha would try to work on him from home. Every day, she drove him to the learning centre. When she picked him up, she would try and talk him through doing his chores. Unfortunately, it never worked. Martha and Conner continued to pray for an answer to their son's irritating behaviour, to no avail. But God works in mysterious ways.

Three weeks after Tristan started going to the learning centre, he had an assignment about Martin Luther King Jr. He learned about how MLK went through trouble and turmoil but never gave up, working as one of the most remarkable civil rights activists in American history. He spoke out against evil and fought for what he believed in, right up until his death. Tristan was stunned; how could one man do so much work and never give up? That night, Tristan talked to his parents about Dr King. He was amazed by how dedicated the activist was.

Tristan was so inspired by Dr King, he decided it was time for him to step up. When his mum asked him if he would clean up the dishes after dinner, not only did he answer yes, but he did it instantly. Amazing, right?

Tristan was finally starting to realise that if he wanted to do good things in life, he needed to stay positive and do good work. Martha and Conner were amazed by this turnaround, and their hearts swelled with pride. They were so glad they didn't give up hope on their son.

Situations like this need faith and hope to overcome them. When dealing with an unruly teen or a disrespectful student - do not give up. Hold on to hope. With patience and love (for your kid and yourself), you will succeed in turning that troubled teenager into a triumphant teenager!

As a parent, you cannot control every little thing your teenager is doing – nor should you want to do it. The teen years are a time when your child is becoming their own person, so they need to have some room to try things out, grow and separate slowly from you. However, as a parent, there are expectations you have of your teenager and things you will and won't allow and it is important that you are clear and consistent about these expectations.

Teens will always push the limits and test you if they know that you are sometimes not consistent. An example of this is Anita, a mother who told her two teens that they could not have friends in the house after school until she got home from work. Anita wanted her children to use this time for doing homework and was tired of coming home to a house full of teenagers who have eaten half the food she bought for the week.

However, the very next day she returned home from work looking to relax and start dinner and there were four other teenagers in the house.

Needless to say, Anita felt disrespected, disappointed and angry. Conflict between parent and teenager was brewing, a perfectly natural occurrence in a world of parenthood and coming-of-age, but that doesn't make it any less frustrating.

Her response was to yell when she walked in the door and told the other teens that they needed to go home. Her children protested repeatedly causing a "scene" in front of their friends which caused Anita to allow them to stay and told them "this was the last time". When it happened the next time, Anita decided that she was going to make it clear that this wasn't OK, and make sure the other teens left and that she did not give into her teen's arguments. When she was clear that they had to leave, her kids then told her that the other teenagers did not have rides home.

This exhausted and frustrated mother then piled the teens in her car and drove them each home to get them out of her house and make her point. When she got back home, she yelled at her children and told them that this was not allowed. Much to her surprise, the next week the same situation happens again. Why? Well, while Anita was telling everyone this behaviour was not allowed, she was actually reinforcing it by not issuing any consequences and then on top of it, driving all the kids home which they probably thought was great. So, what could she have done differently? She called her best friend who suggested to her to do the following:

1. The first suggestion was that she should tell her kids that if they wanted to have all their friends over, they would have to compensate her for all the food and gas in order to deal with their friends. If she put a monetary value on the situation, her teens might be less likely to have people over because it cost money!

2. The second suggestion was that she should tell her kids that if it happens again, she will call the parents of the other teens and explain the situation to them. She will ask them to come pick up their own children. This would likely cause a lot of embarrassment to her children, which is always good leverage. The key is that Anita must follow through with what she says she will do if this happens again.
3. The third suggestion was that she should explore whether there is an adult she can have come to the house after school for a brief period to monitor her teen to make sure no one is coming over. Her teenagers will likely not enjoy this and will feel like there is a babysitter present and may decide it is better to just follow the rules and be home alone.
4. The fourth suggestion was that if this rule is broken again, Anita should look for the consequences that are really powerful for her teenagers and let them know upfront that they would be enforced for any further breaking of this important rule. Anita warned her children that if they broke this rule again that they would lose their phone and video game access for one week.

Again, the most important part is that she follows through

with this consequence if she needs to despite the yelling, badgering and blaming that she may endure from her teenagers. If Anita was consistent, her teenagers would quickly have stopped testing her limits because they would have known that she is serious. Ultimately every one would live in a more peaceful environment where rules, consequences, figures of authority are clear, consistent and predictable.

PUTTING IT INTO ACTION

Curfews are something that all teenagers face and might inevitably hate. As a parent, you should utilise a curfew to give your child freedom, yet show them that you expect there to be boundaries. Curfews are an obvious thing that all teenagers should face, and if a curfew is broken, then there should be consequences that occur once they have disobeyed their set curfew.

For Robin, she didn't see a reason she should have to endure such a curfew. She was good in school, always getting straight A's, and a champion at swimming. She had everything going for her, including many universities/colleges that were already seeking her out. Not to mention, she was one that rarely missed a curfew and thought it was pretty lame that her parents would even invoke such timing for her.

When Robin became friends with Regina, she started to push the limits of when she was coming home. She was driving her parents to wonder how harsh they should be on enforcing the curfew rule. On Saturday nights they set the curfew for 10:00. They didn't think that it was unfair, but Robin began to push the boundaries a little more, mainly to see how lenient her parents might be.

It was going on midnight when Robin walked into the front door. She wasn't really sneaking in, and she didn't think her parents would care all that much. They knew where she was and who she was with, so there was no reason to believe they would make such a big deal about it. However, they were sitting on the living room couch the minute she turned the foyer lights on. She jumped when she saw them. "Oh hey," she said. "I didn't think you'd still be up."

Her dad looked at his watch. "Do you know what time it is?" he asked. Her mom was quick to put a hand on his arm, silently telling him that he shouldn't be quite so hard on her. Robin just laughed nervously. "Yeah, it's midnight, or at least that's what time the radio clock said in Regina's car. Why?".

"Your curfew is for 10:00 pm, did you forget that?" her dad asked. He raised his voice a little, catching Robin off guard. She was a typical teenager, but yet she didn't usually find reasons that her father would yell at her. "No, but you knew I was with Regina and the movie got out late, then we went to get pizza. What's the big deal?". Then her mother stepped forward, most likely wanting to calm the situation. "You don't miss curfew like this and we were worried about you. That's all. We are only just asking that you let us know if you're going to be late from now on".

"That's not it at all," her father interrupted. "You are not to be late because we set a curfew for a reason," he said. "If you're late again, then there will be consequences," he said. Robin's eyes raised. "Consequences? Like what?" she asked. "We will come to pick you up if Regina can't seem to tell time," he said. Robin was mortified that her father would say such a thing. She couldn't imagine either one of them embarrassing her to the point of picking her up off from her friend. A part of her was so sure that they didn't really mean it either, but she didn't know if she wanted to test them like that. She then went to bed feeling a little unsure of things but not thinking too much on it. The next night she went out with her again. This time it was a school night, so she was to be in no later than 10:00 pm. As the time inched closer, she knew they should start heading home, but she was still confident that her parents wouldn't embarrass her and it wasn't like she was going to stay out all night.

It was 10:15. Her parents knew she was going out for ice cream with Regina and sure enough, her father came into the restaurant to pick her up. She felt the embarrassment from the moment he walked up to the table, until the time she said goodbye and left the restaurant with her dad. The whole way home she talked about how ridiculous and unfair it was but all her father kept saying was that she was warned. The concept worked because she never missed curfew again.

So, in the scenario, her parents got their point across that actions have consequences, and they would follow through to make sure she understood that. However, maybe there would have been another option that would have also gotten the point across. How would you have handled it? Would you have followed through with the consequence? What kind of consequences would you offer up, so that it would be a little less embarrassing?

It's crucial that your teenager know that they have rules that needs to be followed, but you want to make sure that your teen isn't scared of you or what you'll do. What could have elicited a better response?

Of course, when taking into consideration the points brought forward in this chapter, you also need to think about everything your teenager is going through. Not only is your teenager likely feeling the frustrations involved with having conflict with their parents (you) but they are experiencing other severe changes in their lives. They may be feeling the effects of issues around a lack of self-awareness or acceptance, confused/mixed emotions around their happiness, frustrations over their social lives and many more complications. It isn't an easy time to be a teenager, especially in the modern, digital world of today.

Always keep that in mind; if it's not smart phones, video games or virtual reality then it's the traditional issues like social life, changing behaviours and unruly attitudes. It's all part of the fun...

5

TEENS AND TECHNOLOGY

We know, we've already discussed technology extensively in this book already, with issues surrounding technology cropping up throughout the various topics we've already honed in on. But, quite frankly, technology today has a much more significant impact on your teenager's behaviour than it would have done ten years ago, or twenty years ago, and is wildly different from thirty years ago [8]. This is why technology deserves its own chapter.

Let's take your first trip to the shop as an example. Your parents likely gave you a very long, well-thought out speech, listing the many guidelines you needed to follow in order to stay safe. Stop at the traffic lights, wait for the green man, don't talk to strangers, follow the yellow brick road. Okay, maybe not the latter, but you get the gist.

Why, then, if we are so cautious about our child's first steps of independence in the real world, are we not even nearly as bothered about their first digital steps on the internet and beyond? It seems baffling that with the growing importance and dependence we have on technology today, that people still don't see that technology and the internet is just as dangerous as the big bad world.

Technology, as we have mentioned, is an ever-changing, ever-developing beast that grows in popularity, usage and accessibility with each day that passes by. Meaning, there are just so many people using internet-enabled digital devices that you can't just assume everybody is a good person. We hate to be the people to break it to you, but the chances are, at least one person you've either communicated with or seen in some form on the internet is likely to be doing something at least slightly illegal. It's weird if you don't come across a weirdo on the internet every now and then. That's why it's more important than ever that both you and your teenager stay safe when trawling the digital realms.

It's not only disingenuous people who have the potential to harm that you need to be careful of either, there are many threats on the internet that don't lead to physical harm - there's emotional scarring, and aspects of the internet that will hurt your purse strings too!

Many young people don't realise that what they see on the

internet may not actually be true, not truly understanding the power and strength of sponsored posts and other such marketing ploys. Particularly relating to those where a reality television star from Love Island or other related programming like Jersey/Geordie Shore, is involved. Many teenagers don't learn to read between the lines until their later teenage years, this is especially the case on social media, where everything you see, on the face of it, appears genuine. As a parent, it can be very harmful for your purse strings if your child is asking for the latest bubble face scrub because Charlotte from Geordie Shore is using it on Instagram. Unfortunately, the teenager doesn't understand that Charlotte doesn't actually like the product, nor does she believe it works, she's just being paid to use it.

The mix of recent technological changes and the ways in which we and those with fame or power engage with social media, combined with normal adolescent developments mean that parenting today is incredibly difficult. Arguably, parenting has never been as difficult as it is today. So, keep in mind that it's hard, your teenagers are living in an age where 'role models' aren't exactly David B and KB anymore, role models are often reality television stars (who are paid an awful lot for not very much work, and often very little talent).

With all this said, there isn't a one-size-fits all guide to how to approach your teenager regarding technology, its ever-changing nature and social media, you instead need to navigate their digital journeys alongside them, as best as you can, without interfering. Piece of cake, right?

Here are some helpful tips and useful nuggets of information that you need to be aware of when it comes to technology:

1. Teenagers are typically absorbed by their social lives - this used to be demonstrated in your teenager nagging to go to their friend's house or go play in the woods. Now, this will be a combination of that and time spent on social media. So, expect to see your teenager's eyes glued to his/her phone almost every minute they're in the house.

Social media, though it seems pointless from your perspective, can actually do some good, we said some... From uploading photos to commenting on viral videos, social media acts as an extension to a real-world friendship, and there are benefits to this.

2. Changes in the brain during adolescence mean teenagers are typically stressed and sensitive in a way that no other age bracket is. This can be demonstrated by them posting a photograph on social media and they only get ten likes instead of twenty. Your teenager may take it personally, they may worry people are beginning to dislike them. This may make them agitated or even add to the mounting stress they are experiencing.

On the subject of uploading photographs and not getting the desired response they were expecting, this may lead to further doubts about their image and therefore could make issues around acceptance and self-love crop up. Social media can be dangerous too.

3. The internet is the perfect storm when it comes to the potential for awful experiences to brew. From snide comments to slut-shaming [9] and nude photo leaks, social media is not only a platform for young people to express themselves, it's a platform for hate-fuelled actions to occur. From a pissed friend to a scorned escort, when something goes wrong with the relationship, watch out, because that person is likely coming for your teenager on social media. And, they won't hold back.

4. You may find solace in discussing the model for a healthy relationship with digital devices and social media with your teenager. Some won't be interested, but it's important for them to be just as aware of the negatives of social media as they are the positives.

5. Highlight the importance of developing good perception and conversation skills. As we mentioned, many teenagers often don't fully acknowledge the power of reading between the lines and often aren't even aware of its very existence. Challenge your teenager to question what he/she sees and not accept everything at face value just because it's commonplace.

6. Build a framework with your teenager that ensures their online activity compliments their offline activity too. Help them to understand that they can't be a different, more confident person online if that isn't going to ultimately reflect on their real world behaviour. Not only can this be confusing for a teenager, it can also help their development.

7. Remind your teenager about the performative aspect of social media and digital device use. Explain why people appear to be happier on social media, when in reality, you have seen them cry many times. Explain why Josh has 4000 friends on Facebook but spends most of his time in his bedroom, hiding away from the real world and real people. Explain why people post pictures of their shopping sprees on the internet. Explain that people project a false version of reality on social media, or at least a lot of people do.

8. With so many social media platforms in existence today, from the 'traditional' Facebook, Twitter and Instagram to the now hugely-popular Tik Tok and Twitch. Social media and content platforms are growing in number and popularity simultaneously, quite frankly it's weird if a teenager doesn't have an online presence today [10]. That said, they're bound to have at least a few followers, or 'friends'. It's important to remind your child that these followers/friends have no reflection on the real life connections they have made with people on a personal, face-to-face basis. Unfortunately, many teenagers believe digital friends are more important, when actually they should be an afterthought.

9. It may be an idea to invite your teenager's friends around to your house. Okay, don't try to be the 'cool' parent, cracking jokes and making your teenager feel embarrassed. Just show them that you're an understanding parent who wants them to be happy and spend time with their friends.

Invite them to the house, get to know them a bit better and ensure your teenager knows that the support network they have in that house at that very moment is the only support network they really need. Anything else is just a nice little bonus.

Graham did this with his son, David. David had been spending far too much time on social media, making friends with other teenagers from different parts of the world who he had gamed with on Xbox Live, playing Fortnite. Graham was concerned that David was forgetting who was in his real support network and chose to remind him in a very real way. He threw a small gathering of friends for David, they all watched TV, ate snacks, played on games and had a good time.

Graham said it reminded David who he really was and who he could turn to when times were tough. David described it as an eye-opener.

10. Ensure that both you and your teenager understand that technology and social media is developing at an unusually fast pace and that nobody really knows where it will be in five years. How technology, the internet and social media will look in ten years would be a complete stab in the dark. Truly, nobody knows. It's for that reason that we need to understand the beast we have mounted in the best way we can before we fully utilise its features.

Things are constantly changing, new threats are introduced with each day that goes by and both parent and teenager need to ensure the safety of each other when using internet enabled devices.

Not only that, but in a few years time it might not be too far out of the realms of possibility for digital devices to enable teleportation - it sounds crazy but technology is advancing so fast. Whether it's through our social media platforms, our emailing systems, virtual reality, or even the way in which we use the internet. Everything is changing, everyday, and if there's something new, you need to understand your child will find it.

LINDA STONE

Technology expert Linda Stone points out that continuous partial attention, or paying a little bit of attention to a lot of stimuli, mimics an ongoing state of crisis—breathing becomes more shallow and the mind hyper-alert. In large doses this behavior can make people feel overwhelmed, overstimulated, and powerless.

Teens are also learning to manage their time—an ability that takes a dip at ages 12-14. Helping them set goals and screen out distractions will help them control their own attention, complete tasks while preserving their energy, and stay in more conscious control of their focus.

PRIORITIZE OFFLINE CONNECTIONS

Young people need secure human relationships to anchor and guide them from infancy through adulthood. These interactions provide validation, information, structure, safety, love, and warmth. Yet both young people and adults say family members spend too much time online at the expense of in-person connections. Emotions expert Barbara Fredrickson believes that in-person relationships affect our physiology differently than online relationships do, increasing our health and ability to connect with others. Kids of all ages say they want parents to turn off devices and tune in to them. Consider enforcing rules like "no phone at the dinner table" or "no phone during homework time" to help your teen focus on schoolwork and family relationships. Likewise, most teens say they prefer face-to-face interactions. Though teens are trying to become autonomous, they also want to maintain close connections and to talk with their parents about things that really matter. They have been telling researchers so for decades.

BALANCE BREADTH AND FOCUS ON INTELLECTUAL DEVELOPMENT

Parents may find it easier to navigate the path of parenthood by taking in as much relevant information as possible about how brains develop so that the children, particularly teenagers are able to learn and emotionally grow independently.

Real-time play and real-life interactions are needed for children to explore, discover cause-and-effect, and lay the foundations of social skills, moral development, self-regulation, agency, and creativity. The skills that as adults, we take for granted on a day to day basis, without ever really taking into consideration just how beautiful the development process itself actually is. In the digital age of today, where social media, peer pressure, defiance and being unhappy in one's skin is commonplace - it's important to reflect on whether or not this affects your child's abilities to build on these foundations. Does it affect it? We're soon to find out.

For this reason, you should be wary of heavy Internet use across all aspects of childhood, but particularly the teenage years. It is much better to expose children to a variety of activities, but obviously this is easier said than done. See, social media particularly is especially detrimental when it comes to body image and confidence, as teenagers, particularly girls, are exposed to bikini-clad women with generally-unattainable figures. When a teenager is developing a sense of who they really are and what they can achieve, social media, among other platforms, can have potentially negative effects on those processes.

Now, this next part may appear complicated on the face of it, but hang in there. By the early teen years, the brain begins a process known as 'specialise'. Unused neurons are pruned for more efficient processing, and the number of connections between them increases. Teen thoughts becomes more abstract, integrated and logical; creativity and competency increases. Whatever teens are doing - from laying around on the couch to editing video projects for school - can become more firmly established in their brains at this time, which makes this a crucial period for learning and developing skills which may change their lives for the better.

For teens, we would suggest supporting their focus on their

emerging interests - including online interests, while still encouraging reflection, analysis, creativity, spaciousness, a quiet mind, and quickness. The more tools, the better. This is a key point to highlight that we are not saying the internet is a bad tool in the development process, but heavy use can hinder development and negatively impact how your teen views themselves, others, and the world around them.

FOSTER EMOTIONAL AND ATTENTIONAL SELF-AWARENESS

Back to the biological side of things... Immaturity of the prefrontal cortex - the part of the brain mostly responsible for self-regulation and decision-making, can make it hard for teens to regulate their emotions and make good decisions. Peer influence, which can also impact good decision-making, is particularly potent between the ages of 12 and 14. Coincidentally, the early teen years are some of the most difficult for parents and the teenagers themselves when it comes to peer pressure. The desire to be popular between these ages can often outweigh common sense or even the morals that come with self-awareness and decency. The immaturity at this age means that for teenagers between the ages of 12 and 14, it can be particularly difficult to differentiate between what your teen actually wants to do, and what their peers are pushing them into.

But teens can be taught emotional skills, like how to take a 'meta-moment' – a pause between being triggered to do something and actually responding - to delay decision-making in order to choose a better path. This is especially important on social media where an impulsive act can have a wide reach and wider consequences. Think back ten or twenty years ago, without the consequences of the modern digital age, without the peer pressure that has become rife on social media, children may have been subjected to peer pressure, but it's nowhere near as harmful or impactful as it is today. Before the internet was as accessible as it is today, children could escape peer pressure by secluding themselves to the comfort of their homes. Now, the peer pressure follows. 'Meta Moment' is therefore crucial in today's modern world.

They can also learn to check in with themselves to become more aware of whether or not hanging out on social media makes them feel connected and happy, or sad and excluded. They can then choose either to maintain the feeling or do something to change it, if social media is not providing them with the connections that they deem necessary.

Take Malcolm, a young teen who spent most of his time posting photos on Instagram. He was a gifted photographer and gained a lot of likes and followers through his photography. Many people commented on his posts, complimenting him for his skill. But Malcolm felt like there was more he could be doing. Even though he had lots of online followers, he didn't really have lots of friends.

One day, Malcolm's art teacher told him about a photography contest held by a local college. He encouraged Malcolm to enter for it. Malcolm took the chance and entered some of his favourite photos into the contest. He won the second place.

During the contest, he made friends with other teen photographers. Many of them used Instagram for posting their pictures, but all expressed the same discontent with the lack of real friends they had online. The teens decided to exchange numbers so that they could communicate and share their work with each other, and make real friends in the process.

After this, Malcolm decided to leave Instagram. He had a good group of friends who would support his photography and critique his work when it is needed to be fixed. He wasn't getting social fulfilment from the application, but with an evaluation of his social media presence, he found a community that was better for his social life. Often, this is the case, and is something that we forget, even as adults. Often seen as a form of escapism where we can engage with our dreams, Instagram, and most other social media platforms are often substituted for actually engaging with that industry in real life. Whether it's because you don't accept yourself and don't believe others will, or you're just not confident enough to push into that real-world network of people, most of us fall into the trap of perusing 'communities' online over actually making connections.

Today's teens must also learn to focus and manage their attention on essential things, instead of being distracted by social media. Technology expert Linda Stone points out that continuous partial attention, or paying a little bit of attention to a lot of stimuli, mimics an ongoing state of crisis—breathing becomes more shallow and the mind hyper-alert. In large doses this behaviour can make people feel overwhelmed, overstimulated, and powerless.

Teens are also learning to manage their time—an ability that takes a dip at ages 12-14. Helping them set goals and screen out distractions will help them control their own attention, complete tasks while preserving their energy, and stay in more conscious control of their focus.

6

COMMUNICATION

Communication is likely the most universally-difficult aspect of life that appears to come so naturally but is so frustratingly hard to get right. Why? Because we all have different expectations when it comes to communication, and it's not just what comes out of your mouth that matters!

Adolescence is a particular time in life where not only is communication especially difficult and frustrating, but is also a time where you don't yet have all the skills necessary to be an effective communicator, or the desire to achieve it - at least not with their parents anyway.

Adolescence is a time of rapid change, not just for the young person but for the parents too. It might be hard to let go sometimes, but parents need to consider the following aspects of parenthood:

- A child's job is to grow up and become an independent adult. Think of it as if they're on a journey through adolescence, but unlike your journey however many decades ago, their journey is everything you experienced alongside the trials and tribulations of the modern, digital age [11]. As a parent, your responsibility is to help your child through the journey, when they need your help, much like your parents did for you as a teenager.
- Decisions can now be made together. Try to discuss issues to reach an outcome that you and your teenager can both accept. In the modern, digital age where your teenager is likely battling issues like peer pressure and self-acceptance, this is going to be much harder than you may realise, but it is possible with effective, clear and well-thought out communication.

Let's take a look at a case from 13 year old Kyle and his father Rufus.

Rufus worked from home, so was always able to keep a record of when his son was out of the home. If Kyle was ever late home from school, Rufus would know about it. One day, Kyle decided to approach the subject of staying out with his friends after school for an hour, rather than trying to go behind his back and lying to him about where he had actually been. Rufus thanked Kyle for bringing the subject to him, rather than using his own free will and going behind his father's back. Due to the mutual respect they had as father and son, Rufus granted Kyle's request, on the condition that he would be back each night before dinner. If Kyle ever missed dinner, Rufus would reassess the situation and there would likely be consequences. Kyle therefore knew not to cross the line, whether it be peer pressure, social media, or just being defiant. Kyle knew that acting out would mean his new-found freedom would be taken away from him - sometimes, that's all it takes.

- Young people may have viewpoints that are different from yours or may decide to explore activities that you don't understand. This is not to say that these activities are out of the ordinary or wrong in any way, but they may be vastly different from your interests. Try to see this as a good thing. They are learning to be their own person. Try to learn more about their interests so you can connect with them on their playing field.
- You will always feel responsible for your child's wellbeing and safety, no matter how old they are.

Yes, even when they're in the forties and complaining that they're finding grey hairs - at least its something you'll be able to relate to. When children reach their teenage years, they start to make their own decisions. Sometimes they make the wrong ones. You should feel slightly responsible, but remember, they're still developing but they're in the awkward phase of wanting independence too. Their wrong actions are predominantly theirs, always keep that in mind.

- Try to be supportive and not critical of them. They will, hopefully, learn valuable lessons from their mistakes. During this time of constant change, both parents and young people need to take time to care for themselves. You need to show you value your teenager, the person they are becoming and their uniqueness – show them your unconditional love.

Let's take a look at a case from 14 year old Shauna and her mother Vanessa. Vanessa was falling into the trap of constantly pointing out that Shauna was always on her mobile phone. Rather than celebrating and supporting Shauna, Vanessa was being overly critical - but she simply thought she was just being a good parent by trying to get her to come off social media. What she didn't realise was that for Shauna, using her mobile phone for social media was her form of escapism after school - she wasn't doing it because of peer pressure, nor was using it manifesting any kind of body issues. Shauna was simply escaping the stresses of school life.

Vanessa, rather than celebrating just how hard working Shauna was and praising her, was focusing too much on Shauna's use of her mobile phone, the one part of Shauna's day where she believed she could just kick back and chill out. Vanessa was being critical and this made Shauna feel as though her efforts weren't good enough and that she was a bad daughter for using social media. From this story, you can learn that there's a different way to approach getting teenagers away from their digital devices - show them there's something better to do, reward positive behaviour with an activity day that they would like - take them away from their mobile phone without them even realising that's what you're doing. Avoid situations of conflict and make sure your child gets the praise they deserve, and criticise only when it's vitally needed as a wake-up call.

GENERAL COMMUNICATION TIPS WITH TEENAGERS

The most important thing is to keep the lines of communication open. Tips include:

- Listen more than you speak: remember that we are

all given two ears and one mouth. This is to remind us that we should spend twice as much time listening as talking. This is especially important when talking to teenagers, who may tell us more if we are silent long enough to give them the opportunity. It's so easy to forget that sometimes the best form of communication is to simply listen to what somebody else has to say. Sometimes, your ears come first, especially when it comes to teenagers. Not only to avoid situations of conflict, but to show your child that you value what they have to say and you care about who they are, their interests and love how God made them.

- Make time for each other together: Meaning, as the parent, you should designate time aside for your teenager, even if they're adamant they don't want to spend time with you - it shows you've thought about them. Teenagers are often busy with school, friends and other interests, but you can have a conversation with them over breakfast and dinner. Offer to take them to or pick them up from places; this will provide other opportunities for conversations. Make superb use of the time you have and build strong connections with the minimal time that you and your teen have together.

Take Stephan for example. An upsetting case of a child who was emotionally neglected, as a teenager he struggled with his body image, representation of men and therefore felt incomplete. He couldn't accept himself in the way that God made him. His parents did not set aside time for him, nor did they offer to drive him to his friends house, in fact, they made little-to-no effort to actually have an in-depth conversation about why he was 'moody' - as they described him. Even if it's just a chat before school over breakfast, put your phone down for a minute and understand that work/your career can wait a minute. Your teenager is more important.

- Give them privacy: Teenagers need their own space. For example, knock before you go into their room. Be prepared for them to want to be alone! In the modern digital age, you may not know what you'll catch them watching or doing otherwise, just a warning…
- Keep up with their interests: As we mentioned earlier, you should embrace your teen's interests, even if they are wildly different from your own. Try to listen to their music, watch their favourite television shows with them and show up to their sports practise sessions. Your teen's preferences may not be yours, but making an effort to take an active interest in their

life will make them feel loved. Not only will this help with their self-confidence but it will also help them to accept themselves and understand that even if their hobbies are unique/niche, they're just as special as any other teenager and there's nothing to be ashamed of - even if it's going trainspotting.

- Be a loving parent: Adolescence is a time when young people often struggle with their changing sense of identity and need to feel loved. Tell them often. Demonstrate your love using whatever physical contact they are comfortable with. Celebrate their achievements, forgive their mistakes, listen to them when they have a problem and show interest in how they plan to solve it. Support them in their problem-solving. Feeling included and special is vital for every young person's sense of positive self-esteem.
- Have fun: make time for leisure and laughter. Good feelings help to build good rapport and connection. Time away from the stresses of modern life is exactly what we all need from time to time - whether it's an escape from peer pressure at school or on social media, or it's a bit of time away from the computer at work. We all need a moment away from reality, nobody is strong enough to be

completely resilient from the trials and tribulations of life.

NEGATIVE COMMUNICATION WITH TEENAGERS

Conflict is inevitable when people with very different viewpoints and experiences in life all live under the same roof, so the occasional clash with your teenager is normal and to be expected. However, ongoing conflict can undermine the relationship between a parent and a young person.

Negative communication is a common cause of prolonged conflict. Examples of negative communication include nagging, harsh criticism, or 'stand over' tactics such as yelling to force compliance.

It's not always easy to recognise negative communication. For example, well-meaning parents may criticise because they want their child to try harder. In the moment, you don't realise it - but you're actually making things worse.

You are using negative communication if:

- The conversation rapidly deteriorates into nagging, yelling or fighting
- You feel angry, upset, rejected, blamed or unloved
- The issue under dispute doesn't ever improve.

Take 15 year old Billy's story as an example. Conflict with his parents was arising so often that he truly believed he was the problem - not an easy achievement for a teenager, even if he wasn't entirely right in his judgement of the situation. It turned out that both he and his parents were using negative communication, which just made everybody unhappy. Not only did Billy feel unloved, his mother felt rejected - so neither of them were emotionally satisfied and his dad was so annoyed that he would often yell. Nobody was winning, as nobody was recognising their communication flaws.

Make sure you do your best to recognise these scenarios and find help to dissolve them if problems persist. Together, you and your teen can create a powerful friendship and bond that all stems from good communication and the ability to make use of the time you are together in your lives. Keep up with their interests, and include them in yours whenever they feel comfortable, but make sure to give them the time they need to make their own decisions and grow into their unique individual with values you have developed in them earlier.

PUTTING IT INTO ACTION

Edward was a hard-working man that rarely was home much to spend time with his wife and his son. On the rare occasion that he had, he tended to find himself angry with his son over his choices in TV and Music, mostly wanting to pull Charlie onto his side of thinking.

As a teenager, Charlie wanted nothing to do with that, but it always caused rifts in their relationship. One night when Edward walked into Charlie's room, he attempted to talk to his son, but his son's music was blaring on the speaker in his bedroom. Needless to say, good intentions seemed to fall a little bit flat, when Edward's old ways came crashing back in.

Edward cleared his throat, attempting to get Charlie's attention. Since the music was blaring so long, playing words that he couldn't even understand, the clearing of the throat went unheard.

"Could you turn that down?" he yelled over the beating of the music that was playing. Charlie stared at him, a blank look on his face. "Huh?" he hollered out. It was no wonder that Charlie couldn't comprehend what his father was saying, no one would be able to hear over the loud sound playing through the speakers.

"Turn it down!" he yelled again, this time making it a little louder, to the point where Charlie heard him. Charlie just laughed.

"It's how the kids play it nowadays," Charlie stated.

"I want to talk to you, and you can't even understand the

words I'm saying," his father argued.

Charlie rolled his eyes and leaned over to turn down the music. "What do you want to talk about?" he asked. Edward was and remain at a loss for words as he didn't really have anything planned out. "You should stop listening to the music so loud. It'll hurt your ears."

Charlie laughed. "Good one Dad." He started to lean over to turn it back up, but Edward stopped him. "I'm serious. Give it a rest. Your mom and I aren't interested in hearing the music, and neither are the neighbours."

"You never are," Charlie mumbled. It was low enough that Edward didn't quite catch on to what it was.

"What'd you say?" he asked. "Nothing Dad," he said. "Can you please just leave? It's not like I'm hurting anyone." "You should be doing more beneficial things with your life, than listening to that...that..." he bit his tongue, letting the words fall off, but Charlie knew what he wanted to say. He rolled his eyes. "Just because it is not your cup of tea, doesn't mean it's all bad. It's not all about what you want."

"What's that supposed to mean?" Edward asked. Charlie heaved a sigh. "Nothing! Do you want anything else?" he asked, clearly annoyed. "No. Just keep it down." Edward turned to leave, and he heard Charlie say something, but by the time he was going to inquire what it was, Charlie had turned the music up. It wasn't quite as loud but loud enough. Edward shook his head and left the room. He would have another talk another day.

Edward obviously wasn't getting through to Charlie. He didn't agree with Charlie's choice of music for one, that was the first roadblock between them, but it only escalated from there. What could Edward have done to get a better response from his son? It's not about proving to your child that you're right and they are wrong, but communication is vital to any given relationship.

Let's see how Edward hands a new tactic and see if it gains better communication between the father and son. The music was blaring as Edward walked into Charlie's room. He walked over to the audio system and automatically turned it down a little, causing Charlie to show his sign of surprise. "What'd you do that for?" he asked.

"I need to talk to you and thought we could take a minute with a little less noise." The music was still playing, but the decrease was apparent. At first, Charlie didn't seem pleased, but he didn't argue. "Okay. What do you want to talk about?"

Edward motioned to the audio system. Charlie thought and figured that he was going to start yelling about how it was so loud, but Edward didn't do that. "Okay…" he stated. "Who's the band?" he asked. "Catfish And The Bottlemen, why?" he asked. Edward shrugged. "Just curious. It's a catchy tune." Charlie chuckled. "Really? You think so?" Edward nodded. "Can't much understand the words, but I'm guessing that's because I don't know the lyrics. Perhaps if I was familiar with them, then it would be different." "Uh yeah...perhaps," Charlie said. "Are they your favourite group?" Edward asked.

Charlie shrugged. "Pretty much I guess. I like the latest stuff they have out. You should hear it sometime. I think you'd like it."

Edward smiled. "Maybe I would." He dragged a chair and sat down, the music still playing in the background. "How's everything else going? School? Track? Oh, and your mom said you wanted to try out for wrestling. When's that?"

Charlie was beaming by this point. He immediately started to rattle off the information his dad asked, leading into the most in-depth conversation that they had had in a long time. Edward was glad he decided to go into Charlie's room.

Once communication started, it seemed to flood out of them, and that's sometimes all it takes. They were both left feeling good about the interaction, and no one had reason to argue or scream at one another. Good, honest, and open communication with your teen will help you form a bond that will only strengthen into adulthood. It's the impressionable years that you don't want to waste.

BUILDING GOOD CHARACTER

Remember when you were a teenager? You probably had to juggle school, family time, and maybe even a part-time job. Your parents probably did their best to ensure that you stayed out of trouble, and it's likely that they did a good \job of imparting some important life skills to you.

Now, you're a parent yourself, and you are faced with the problem of how to provide your teens with the life skills they need to face the future head on [12]. Not only that, but you're battling alongside the modern day stresses that the digital world has presented to us, in the form of social media and the widely accessible internet at your fingertips, presenting a whole host of issues from self-doubt and body issues, all the way up to peer pressure and rising conflict in the household.

You want to help your teenager build good character traits that benefit themselves and the people around them. You didn't know it then, but your parents were struggling with this same issue when you were younger. They made it through this troubling time, and you will too.

There are many things you can do to ensure that your teen is heading in the right direction. Let's take a look at just a few important traits your teen will need as a young adult, and talk about ways you can help your kids learn valuable lessons that will help them now and in years to come.

Independence

It is natural for teenagers to long for independence. Think back to your own teenage years - didn't you have a longing for freedom? Didn't you want to make your own decisions? Your kids are the same way. They want to make their own choices and they dream of leaving their mark on the world. It may be worth asking yourself how old you were when your parents gave you your first experience of independence, whether it was a bus journey into town with your friends or going to the cinema without them. Ask yourself if you were old enough or you felt you could have done with building on your maturity, this will help to inform you on how best to develop your teen's sense of independence and at what age to do it.

Fostering independence in your teenager is important. Even though you may worry about what your kids are doing when you're not around, you've got to let them gain that important sense of self-worth that comes from being trusted to be alone. They also need to learn the consequences, positive or negative, of their actions and how to handle them on their own. Be sure your teenagers know what is and isn't acceptable as activities. Never give them a reason to hide anything from you, and never make them feel that they can't come to you with problems. If they slip up, come up with a plan for dealing with the problem effectively — use negative incidents as tools for growth, instead of falling into despair. If you think about it, most of us have made mistakes!

Take Gina's situation. She was given her first opportunity for independence when her parents allowed her to take the bus into the city centre with her friends. One of her friends was caught shoplifting and though Gina didn't directly steal anything herself, she maintained the story that her friend was innocent - despite CCTV footage showing otherwise.

When Gina's parents found out, they were livid. They told Gina that no matter who it is, she should know the difference between right and wrong. Rather than telling her what to do next, Gina came to the conclusion herself. She apologised to her parents for lying and said she only did so because she thought her friend was going to be in serious trouble. She confirmed that she now knew it wasn't the right thing to do in the moment. Gina learnt the consequences of her negative actions so she could learn from that situation in case it ever arose again.

Don't let worry stand in the way of growth. Gina's parents didn't. Giving your kids a sense of independence doesn't mean that you're abandoning them, or turning them out into the world completely unprepared for reality. You can teach this life skill by gradually encouraging independent thinking, and by providing teens with opportunities to make the right choices. If you don't do this, you are doing your teen a disservice!

Your kids will become adults one day - and it will happen sooner than you think. Isn't it great to know that when you provide them with a sense of confident independence, you are also giving them a greater chance to be happy and successful in life?

Responsibility

Everyone has responsibilities. If your kids have no responsibilities now, then it is time to do them a favour, and give them something to be responsible for. Make the first responsibility you give your teenagers small ones. Perhaps it can be up to them to set the table for dinner, or to sort and fold their own laundry. Maybe they need to learn to make their own beds or pick up after themselves. Household chores are great ways to build responsibility and prepare your teen for when they're living on their own.

If they have already graduated from simple tasks like this, then they are ready for bigger responsibilities. They may be ready to start earning some money on their own. Perhaps they are ready to look for small business opportunities, or maybe they can be responsible for helping younger kids with their homework. If they're old enough, you might also consider teaching them how to drive a car. Being a responsible citizen is one of the most significant traits your teen can build. Make sure that greater amounts of responsibility are met with greater rewards, and be sure that the rewards are meaningful. Talk about positive and negative consequences, and be sure that your teen knows that he or she is ultimately responsible for things that happen in the future.

When Danny turned sixteen, he wanted nothing more than to have a car of his own. He had already taken all of the driver's education courses he needed and was well on his way to getting his driver's license. However, his parents weren't sure he was responsible enough to have his own vehicle. Cars were a significant investment and could cause a lot of harm if owned by an irresponsible person. They told Danny he needed to prove his responsibility to them before they would consider getting him a car. Danny talked to his counsellor about it, and he suggested that Danny should tutor younger students in history. It was Danny's favourite subject, and he knew a lot about it. He was unsure about it, though, because he had never tutored anyone before. It was, after all, a considerable responsibility for him to take up! On the first day of tutoring, Danny was still unsure. He had two students asking about the Revolutionary War. He helped them study for their upcoming test by quizzing them about significant battles and important figures. The next week, the students came back and told him they passed their test with flying colours!

Danny was incredibly pleased and continued his work at the tutoring centre. His parents were happy too. He was helping out his community and sharing his knowledge with students! Danny proved to them that he was responsible, and they sat down with him to start the process of buying a car.

Making the Most of Relationships

If your teenager spends more time watching TV, or has their eyes glued to social media, or they just love playing video games more than they spend involved in meaningful activities that foster real-life relationships, then you may have the beginning of a problem on your hands. Of course, in the digital age of today, this is probably more likely to be the case than not, unfortunately, and is why you need to make the most of the relationship you have with your teenager, and the relationships he/she has with other people.

Kids who don't learn how to interact effectively with other people and shy away from opportunities tend to do poorly once they are out on their own. When you're so used to the interaction of a quick 'like' or a 'comment', it can be hard to be fluid when shifting between digital and real life correspondence, especially if you're still learning how to communicate.

One of the most important character traits for teenagers involves interpersonal interaction with people from various walks of life. You could encourage your teens to get involved with sports, or to participate in youth group activities sponsored by your church or community centre. Kids can learn a lot by shadowing adults at work, and they can even mentor smaller children once they have gained some experience. What matters most is that they are involved. Face to face interactions are crucial in their development into an adult. While it is true that computers and other electronics devices are here to stay, the need to interact with others in professional and social ways will never go away. Do all you can to be sure that your teens are learning how to create balanced relationships with other people. When it comes to intimate relationships, be sure to give your children the education they need, and to avoid being mislead.

Teens must know that attraction to others is a natural phenomenon to experience once they reach 12 and 13 years old. With TV and the internet, sometimes children begin experiencing attraction at an early age. This must be addressed at an early age so that positive understanding can be modelled. If teens don't understand what's going on and lack the guidance to navigate this hard time, they may give into dangerous practices and unhealthy actions. When they deny it they become stronger, but if they give in to every desire of theirs, they become a slave of that desire.

If you are too close with someone of the opposite sex, it is like holding two polarised magnets together. How far can you hold two magnets together without it touching? It will always touch when you bring them close. If they are far away you can keep them apart but the closer you bring them together the attraction is very strong. This can be what happens when two teens are attracted to each other and have no guidance on how to deal with relationship.

It is important for teenagers to understand that intimacy is more than just physical contact. If you are not sure about how to approach this subject with your teens, you're not alone. This is one of those life skills for teenagers that can be tough to approach effectively! Luckily, there are many books and other

resources that can help you to provide your teenager with the skill and courage to follow the straight and narrow path to healthy relationships. Study these to learn how to effectively tackle these challenging subjects, as they are essential and can't be forgotten.`

PREPARING YOUR KIDS FOR LIFE IN THE REAL WORLD

Once your teenagers become adults, they will need to do all kinds of things from how to change a tyre on a car, all the way up to how to budget correctly when they move out and get their own place. They will need to be able to manage money effectively, and they will need to be able to make good decisions when it comes to things like buying a car, using debit cards, making decisions about who to spend their time with, and how to use that time most effectively.

One way you can encourage positive character traits and functional life skills is by modelling them yourself. Take a good look in the mirror: Are you the kind of person you would like your son or daughter to grow up to be? If not, you might want to take steps to become the individual you wish to and dream your teen will one day become. If you don't believe you're a good enough example of somebody your children can look up to, inform your children honestly and openly of how you could have done better - teach them the lessons they're going to need to know.

PUTTING IT INTO ACTION

Stacey was a bright student that always strived to do her best in school. Her mother, however, had become worried about her because it seemed like the only thing Stacey was interested in was studying and possibly reading in her spare time.

To many parents that might have been a dream come true for them, but to Veronica, she was still concerned about her daughter. Veronica was a single parent, having divorced Stacey's father when she was just a toddler. She had never been remarried and never went into another relationship after the divorce, as she really only had time to work and tend to her teen. Part of her wondered, if maybe Stacey had picked up on Veronica's lack of social circles because she never saw her daughter hanging out with many friends or doing anything beyond studying and reading.

She decided that she needed to take things into her own hands and that meant changing the way Stacey saw her mother interacting with those outside of their home. One day, Veronica decided to make it happen. Veronica walked into her daughter's bedroom, and Stacey had a book in hand, lying on her bed, while the book was propped up on her knees. She barely even noticed when her mother walked in until Veronica made a slight noise. Stacey looked up. "Hey," then went back to reading. "Reading anything interesting?" Veronica asked.

Stacey shrugged. "Reading a new book that Mrs Brewster introduced to us. It's pretty interesting."

Veronica, who knew much about what was going on with her daughter and school, knew that Mrs Brewster was her English teacher. "That's nice." She hesitated before adding the latter part. "I want you to come with me somewhere." Stacey looked up, obviously intrigued. "Where?" she asked. "I know a co-worker that has a daughter about your age. She invited us out for supper." Stacey groaned and started to make up a million excuses why she couldn't go. Veronica had heard them all, including the fact that she had said many of them too. However, she wasn't going to let Stacey out of this one. It would do them both a bit of a good. "It will only be a couple of hours out of the night. You can come back and read again another time. Just do this for me. Will you?"

Being a single parent, they had a pretty good relationship, so Stacey agreed, even though she knew in her mind she didn't want to do it. If it was going to make her mom happy, then she would. They left and went to the restaurant where

Mallory and Megan already were. The minute they got there, Veronica worried that maybe she had moved too fast for Stacey. Megan was bubbly, outgoing, and the complete opposite of her daughter. Fifteen minutes in, though after they all had ordered what to eat and drink, it seemed like Stacey and Megan were getting along well. It relieved Veronica, giving her less and less time to worry and more time to talk to Mallory.

The dinner went well, showing Veronica that it was good for both of them. They decided to set up another time to get together, and even Megan and Stacey were talking about hanging out together sometime after school. When they got in the car, Stacey turned to her mom. "Thank you. That was fun," she said.

Veronica smiled and had to agree. It didn't hurt for her to get out there and actually do something for a change that didn't include work. She even looked forward to going out again. So as stated earlier, evaluate yourself and see if

there are ways you can change to make things better on how your son or daughter interacts. If Stacey hadn't gone out to the restaurant, she would have still been stuck in her room, instead of finding new friends to add to her social network.

Present interactions can determine the future for you, and you should never shy away from that.

LIFE SKILLS THAT EVERY TEENAGER SHOULD LEARN

There are several skills in life that individuals should learn to help them manage the trials and challenges that they may experience while reaching for their dreams. For teenagers, these life skills will help them be more mature and independent. The skills will also promote good habits and responsibility. As parents, we play a crucial role in helping our children learn these skills.

MONEY MANAGEMENT SKILLS

Knowing how to budget and manage money is one of the most essential and challenging skills to master, so it is vital to help your child understand the basics of this from a young age. It may seem like a difficult task, especially when your teenager is already battling everything from peer pressure to body issues but it is achievable if you go about it the right way.

Parents should teach their children the proper way of budgeting their money so that they can have enough money to pay for their monthly expenses, as well as to save money to be used for special purposes or in case of an emergency. It is also important that parents educate their teenage son or daughter about the difference between wants and needs. One of the easiest ways to learn to budget is to have self-discipline on what items are necessary to have, and which ones would just be nice to have. By educating them in the difference between 'want' and 'need', you can guide them in the right direction.

Teenagers also need to know how to balance their checking accounts, set their financial priorities, and to pay bills. These are skills that can be grown over time in small steps. Giving them a clear insight of what the real world is all about is crucial in instilling them with a sense of importance regarding their finances.

Katherine gave her kids a weekly allowance in exchange for doing their chores. Whenever she paid them, her daughter Esther would go out and spend it all immediately. Esther wanted to save up money for the xbox X (it isn't even out yet, that's how eager she was) but kept spending her allowance on food and soft drinks. She would then complain when her mother told her she wouldn't pay for the system. Esther wanted the best of both worlds - and as adults, we know that can't always be the case.

Finally tired of telling her daughter no, Katherine sat her down and showed her daughter how she usually budgeted for the week. She divided up her paycheck so that every week she was putting money into her savings account. Then, she'd pay off her loans, debts, or credit card bills she had. With the money she had left she would prioritise buying food and basic supplies for the week. When she wanted to buy a nice, more expensive product, she would draw some money out of her savings account.

Esther decided to set up her own savings account and started to put away some of her allowance each week. It took a while, but she was able to buy the game system she wanted. She also learned essential values from her mother, that would later grow and help her develop a more fruitful life.

TIME MANAGEMENT SKILLS

Every teenager must learn how to use their time wisely so that they can accomplish more things. Time management enables teenagers to complete the tasks and responsibilities before the set deadlines. It also prevents them from experiencing stress and anxiety. Another benefit of time management is that it helps children make better decisions. Helping your teens with their time management skills will pay dividends for the rest of their lives, and is one of the most critical skills you can teach your growing young adult.

Parents can teach their teenage son or daughter how to properly manage their time by being a good role model and providing them the necessary tools to develop such skills. It would also help if they encourage teenagers to create a schedule of the things that they need to accomplish for the day and even for the week. They should also encourage their children to develop a routine.

Take the story of Natasha and her daughter Freya. Natasha always stressed the importance of having good time management skills by working her fingers to the bone to maintain a high level of efficiency. She would set reminders on her iPhone for everything. She would have Alexa give her reminders just in case anything went wrong with her iPhone. She had a routine for everything and always did things on time - it was exhausting, but it meant she got to teach her daughter efficiency, productivity and good time management skills.

Learning to develop routines can take a long period of time, but it can be incredibly rewarding. Not only can it motivate your teenager into behaving in the same way you do but it can also give them the kick they need to be productive, participate in activities and engage with the world around them.

Take Dave, who used to be incredibly unorganised and messy. His mom was often frustrated when he stayed up late the night before a project was due because he hadn't started it yet. He came home one afternoon and told her about an English paper he had to write. When she asked him when he was going to start, he shrugged. She decided to sit him down and outline the writing process so he could get it done before the due date. For the first week, it didn't work. But when the second week started, Dave found out there was a cool concert happening the day before the essay was due. His mother told him he could go if he got his paper done before the show.

Dave's essay was supposed to be five paragraphs, with quotes for evidence. He spent his first-day finding quotes and writing the introduction. The second day he wrote the next two paragraphs, and the third he wrote the last two. By sectioning out his time, he was able to get the paper done early and go out to the concert. He didn't like it at first, but once he realised there would be consequences for his actions, he started to schedule his time out.

Working with teens for an extended period of time has lots of value; if his mom hadn't kept encouraging him to manage his time, he wouldn't have grown positively.

HOUSEHOLD MANAGEMENT SKILLS

Teenagers should learn how to do household jobs such as cooking, doing the laundry, shopping for foods, and cleaning the house. If they are going to move out and live on their own one day, they need to learn these basic skills. Parents can start teaching their teenagers about these skills by assigning them with household chores that they can do for a week, starting small and gradually getting bigger as they gain experience and discipline.

One great way to do this is to have a family meal once a week where your teen helps cook dinner. Teens learn through practice and repetition. The more often they do something, the easier it will come to them. Not only that, but in the modern, digital age of today, it is so easy to implement - as anybody can follow the simple instruction of Alexa reading from a recipe from the internet.

If you involve your teenager in cooking dinner, they'll get better with time and learn a valuable life skill. As an added reward, you get to spend time with your teen and engage in great conversations. Aside from basic household skills, teenagers must also learn good hygiene skills and habits. They should be able to keep their bodies clean and their environment hygienic. Parents should educate their children about the importance of having a regular exercise schedule, eating healthy foods, and having enough sleep.

GOAL SETTING SKILLS

Teenagers must learn how to set goals and develop strategies to achieve them. It is important that parents advise their children to only set realistic goals. It would be better if they help them clarify specific goals and share some techniques on how to achieve them. Realistic goal setting pushes teens to better themselves and can help them increase their sense of self-worth and esteem. This is a time when social media is particularly harmful - as it can often set unrealistic expectations and goals for young people.

Brian was a busy student. He was the goalie for the football team, part of the school drama club, and spent time in the tutoring centre as he tried to improve his essay writing. His parents were proud of him, but sometimes it felt like he was going to exhaust himself! In his junior year, he wanted to be the lead in the school play and the captain of the soccer team. However, he also had a big essay assignment that was due the week of the fall play. Nora, Brian's mother, suggested he set more realistic goals. Instead of achieving all three, he needed to prioritise his activities.

Brian decided to start by setting the goal of getting at least a

B+ on his essay. To do that, he scheduled appointments at the tutoring centre once a week. He then determine to try out for the school play, but for a part as one of the side characters. He could still have an important role that didn't require as much practice. Finally, twice a week, after soccer practice, he dedicated time to doing extra exercises. He knew that if he worked slowly, he could be made captain by his senior year!

PROBLEM SOLVING SKILLS

Every individual have their own problem. These problems can create a considerable impact on the lives of various individuals when not handled properly. In the modern, digital age of today, it's highly likely that your teenager is going to run into a whole hosts of problems from peer pressure to online bullying.

Teenagers need to learn how to think of possible solutions to different types of problems on their own. Teenagers with good problem solving skills can handle any problem that life has to offer. Teaching your teenagers how to deal with everything from interpersonal relationships to money management can be tough, but there are plenty of fantastic resources available to help you accomplish the task! So, think about the individual challenges you and your teenager face, and then get started. Each day that passes without action on your part brings your teen a day closer to adulthood. By ensuring that your teenager has the life skills he or she needs, you are helping to provide a better future.

Carla's son Logan usually came to her when he was struggling with something. They had a good relationship, so Carla was surprised when Logan came home from school and slammed the door to his bedroom. She knocked on the door and tried to ask him what was wrong, but he didn't answer. She gave him space in hopes he come and talk to her later.

At dinner, Logan explained that his friend John was mad at him but didn't tell why. John froze Logan out all day and didn't want to sit with him at lunch. Carla was sympathetic; this happened to her once or twice when she was his age. Carla asked him how he thought he would solve the problem. Logan wasn't sure. John refused to talk to him, so how could he know what was wrong?

Carla knew she couldn't do anything from home, so she suggested he ask a school counsellor for help. Logan agreed it would help; if he could have a mediated discussion with John, they could talk out the problem. At school, John and Logan sat down with a school counsellor. John finally admitted he was mad that Logan had aced his maths test, while John failed it again. Logan knew he was better at maths than John was, but didn't help his friend. Even though it wasn't actually his fault, Logan felt terrible. He decided that in order to resolve their issue, he would try and tutor John in maths. John was hesitant, but after seeing how much his friend cared about him, he agreed. This way, Logan was able to save his friendship and teach his friend the maths problem - solving skills he needed to pass.

It's safe to say that in the world we live in today, where everything around us is constantly changing, you need to teach your child a variety of vital skills that they will always need, regardless of technological advancements, so that they can survive.

Please Leave a 1-click Review!

Thank you for reading this book and engaging in the next step to establishing positive life strategies. I hope this book helped you in the same way it has helped many others.

I would really appreciate a short review for this book. Your help in spreading the word is greatly appreciated. Reviews from readers like you make a huge difference to helping new readers find helpful books like this one. I joyfully read every single review.

Just click on the link below and you will be taken straight to the review page on Amazon. Thank you!

Review Book Here

LAST WORD

The world we live in today, the digital world we have referenced throughout this book is a very complex world, a very toxic space too. Unfortunately, our children are about to inherit it from us, and who knows what it will become. See, the world today is changing at an alarming rate, being much different from how it was just five years ago, and completely unrecognisable from how it was just fifteen years ago. Technology is ever-changing and evolving, trends are becoming ever more materialistic and who knows what is to come after the digital age.

With all the uncertainty, and knowing just how difficult it must be to grow up in a world where your mobile phone isn't just a device, it's a lifeline, we need to approach things differently to how your parents may have done when you were a child. We need to own the situation we find ourselves in, upgrade our thinking, and re-connect with our heart and soul.

We have to apologise for our failings and ask for forgiveness as steps to heal the chasm between us. We need to model the behaviour that we expect from them. If we want them to tell the truth, then we must. If we want them to respect us, then we must treat them with respect as we guide them and set limits for them. Think of it like your teenager is on a tour bus in a foreign land and you're the tour guide - but the only thing is, the city you're describing is changing simultaneously as you're teaching your 'audience'. It's a difficult task made even harder by the ever-changing landscape of the modern, digital age where so many aspects of modern life can affect the development of your teenager.

If we want our teenagers to have compassion, then we must create the experience of compassion from ourselves to them. If we want them to understand us, then we need to understand them. Whatever we want and are asking from our teens, we need to be that. Our behaviour will be an influence for good to show them the way to move from adolescence into the maturity that adulthood needs to be.

Our teens need us to get off our phones and iPads, turn off the TV, the computer, and other distractive technology and activities same with limit setting. Because, let's face it - sometimes we can be just as glued to our devices as our teenagers are!

We can't be a model for them when we are doing the same things we tell them not to do. "Do as I say not as I do" teaches lying, manipulation and deception It is time that we stop and smell the flowers. The world today is not what it was years ago, but we are still trying to educate and care for our children the way our parents did. They know more about the world than we will ever know.

There's no more room for lies or for excuses because they have seen it all, and many times they have lived through it. This is the time when we must try desperately to get close to them, to talk to them, to reach for them and make huge efforts to understand what they are going through every day. We must be patient, we must be ready to hear everything without being judgmental, give them love and not punishment, they are already being punished by society itself.

It is our duty to make our homes a place of peace, a place where they can open up and speak of their pain, their problems, their doubts and fears. You and I have both sat before our children and heard stories of things that happened at school or anywhere else and they seem so wild and crazy that they do not register in our minds. We react negatively to their stories and call them liars. But many of these stories and excuses are true and they live through them every day. The time has come to arm ourselves with patience and with tons and tons of love. It is time for us to serve our teenage children as anchors, as forts where they feel safe away from all the pain and suffering their world is made of.

Take the time to pray and speak with them a few minutes every day. Ask them about their day, how they feel, about school, or anything at all. The point is to work on opening communication channels. You need to learn about their interests. Watch their favourite shows, learn about their friends, and get involved with them. If you spend as little as ten to fifteen minutes every day just talking with your child, you are making an investment in giving them a better, safer life. They are the most precious parts of our lives, learn about them, watch them, share with them, soon they will be adults themselves and will go their own ways.

Now is the time to establish a true relationship with your teenager, not tomorrow, not next week, or not when you think they might want to talk. Actively seek to grow with your teenager and be the best 'tour guide' you can be. Don't wait until later on, as the opportunity will have passed and it is impossible to reverse time and the consequences of our not paying attention when attention was needed.

Think back to the stories of Gina, Stacey, Billy and Kyle. Our teenagers need our help, even if they don't like to admit it. Put your cap on, brave a smile and jump on that 'tour bus', because you're about to give the best performance of the parent/teenager journey through the modern digital age.

OTHER BOOKS YOU'LL LOVE!

CLICK ON THE BOOKS

Link to Book

126 | OTHER BOOKS YOU'LL LOVE!

[Link to Book](#)

[Link to Book](#)

OTHER BOOKS YOU'LL LOVE! | 127

[Link to Book](#)

[Link to Book](#)

128 | OTHER BOOKS YOU'LL LOVE!

Link to Book

Link to Book

OTHER BOOKS YOU'LL LOVE! | 129

Link to Book

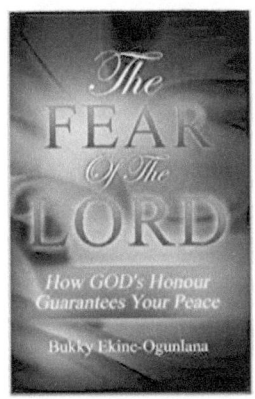

Link to Book

130 | OTHER BOOKS YOU'LL LOVE!

[Link to Book](#)

REFERENCES

1. https://www2.ed.gov/parents/academic/help/adolescence/adolescence.pdf
2. https://kidshealth.org/en/parents/talk-about-puberty.html
3. https://www.youngpeopleshealth.org.uk/wp-content/uploads/2015/07/533_Mental-health-RU-Feb-2014-public.pdf
4. https://www.webmd.com/depression/guide/untreated-depression-effects#1
5. https://kuclinic.ku.edu/sites/kuclinic.ku.edu/files/files/Negative%20Behavior%5B1%5D%20copy.pdf
6. http://www.sdparent.org/web/site_2825_files/files/1381413101_Picking_Your_Battles_Presentation.pdf

7. https://childmind.org/article/tips-communicating-with-teen/
8. https://core.ac.uk/download/pdf/58825115.pdf
9. https://www.researchgate.net/publication/233217252_Slut-shaming_girl_power_and_'sexualisation'_Thinking_through_the_politics_of_the_international_SlutWalks_with_teen_girls
10. https://www.researchgate.net/publication/270161373_Teens_social_media_use_and_collective_action
11. https://www.researchgate.net/publication/324694265_PARENT_-_TEENAGER_COMMUNICATION_IN_THE_DIGITAL_ERA
12. https://parentandteen.com/building-character-in-teens-one-of-the-7-cs-of-resilience/

FINANCIAL TIPS TO HELP KIDS

PROVEN METHODS FOR TEACHING KIDS MONEY MANAGEMENT AND FINANCIAL RESPONSIBILITY

INTRODUCTION

It's a universal search, don't we all agree, the search for money. It's part of why we are on a job, isn't it? We work to earn money, not just money in itself, but for what money can procure for us.

As a means of exchange, even from ancient times, money has always been one of the most elusive things the world over. Most people are in endless search for money. Grab some, and you see the need to seek more, then more, and more of money to exchange for the increasing material things we require in modern time to lead a comfortable life.

It is however increasingly becoming the case that the problem with most people isn't the complete lack of money or insufficient fund, but the mismanagement or abuse of money. And the result is never pleasant for anyone.

INTRODUCTION

Generation after generation, we have seen mistakes and errors repeated regarding how people treat money, leaving the vast majority of people poor, impoverished, deprived and destitute.

I'd like to see a change.

Don't you?

My kids have got to make a difference after I've taught them how to relate with money. I believe the desire for most parents is mutual. We should all be teaching our kids about money. And starting early is key. We don't want them making grievous mistakes or setting off in life knowing nothing about how to grow finances, or treating money with disrespect.

I needed to be certain that parents have the right knowledge with which to equip their children from early in life with viable and sustainable financial tips. It's a very important responsibility kids can learn. They need to know how to account for and manage money.

Oh! Have we heard and seen examples of kids who do not understand the concept of money management or how to handle money to impact their quality of life? It's important for adults to teach kids these lessons which can positively impact the rest of their lives.

After reading this guide, please feel free to leave a review based on your findings and how useful the guide was to you. It is always important to hear feedback, so please feel free to leave a helpful review and if you feel like it warrants it, recommend the guide to your friends and family.

1

FINANCE FOR KIDS

It's never too soon to start teaching children about finances. It can be hard to talk to kids about money. You may have to acknowledge your own mistakes, and potentially even inject a sense of reality into your wide-eyed offspring. And the economic situation of society today continues to worsen, with the gap between the rich and the poor getting wider, it is more important nowadays than ever before to teach the importance of managing your finances, as early as possible.

DAN'S MUM'S APPROACH

Dan walked up to his mum and requested for £5 for materials for his school project. She knew how important the project was for him and that he needed to get a good grade, but she also needed to make him understand the value of money. So she started by asking him, "What can you do to earn this money you are asking from me?"

Amazed that such question could come from his mum, Dan said: "Mum, seriously? Can't I just have it?"

His mother replied, "You need to know the difference between earning something and getting it on a platter."

Dan was rapt in attention now. He did not only show affirmation but respect for his mum. In engaging with his mother and getting a clear, firm answer, he was able to gain a clearer insight into what the real world is like - where you need to work for the things you want, and the things you don't necessarily even want but need to survive.

"When you work to get something done," the mum continues, "how will you handle it?"

Dan replied "Of course, I'll handle it well, mum. I won't allow any scratch on it."

"Do you know how important it is to do a good job?" she asked.

"Yes, otherwise you won't get repeat business." Dan quipped.

His mum proudly answered, "You're learning, good."

"When I return from school today, I'll help pick up your items from the grocery store," Dan offers.

"Now, you earn it with respect," she told him and gave him a loving hug as she tucked the £5.00 in his hands.

That was all she did to infuse in Dan the understanding of the value of money and how to handle it.

TALKING ABOUT MONEY

Talking to your children about money is important [1]. It's difficult to know when to have the 'money talk' with your children, as all parents are difficult. The first real talk about work and money should happen long before your child has their first bank account, or at least before they are aware of what a bank account even is. That way, you establish the idea that you only spend money that you have earned. This helps to inculcate a sense of fiscal responsibility in your child. Turn everyday's activities into teaching moments. When you go shopping, talk about comparing prices, looking for good deals, and how prices go up and down. If you drop by the cash machine, explain that you have to fund your bank account in order to take money out of the cash machine. When you pay your bills, talk about how debit/credit cards work, and about debt and interest. As your children get older, talk about the importance of insurance, and its costs.

If you are having an especially difficult time getting the conversation started, consider online resources, alongside thorough use of this guide, taking the information that works for you and utilising it alongside other materials and online tools. In society, we're often taught about the 'taking' side of finances but not so much about the significance of giving back. Get your children involved in the process of donating to charity would therefore likely be a wise thing to do. Allow them to choose who they give to out of their own conviction, and doing so willingly, sacrificially and joyfully. Not only does this give them a sense of importance and new-found confidence, it allows them to research charities and find one that means something to them.

Encouraging children to work is also a crucial aspect of your child building a solid framework of their personal finances. Working can teach your child valuable life's lessons. Even if your kid is too young to work, set up an allowance system in which they have to complete certain tasks in order to receive rewards. Create a budget for the things you provide. Make categories such as clothing and electronics, and allow them to decide whether to spend or save for higher quality items. Set up a checking and *savings* account, and reward them for saving.

When your child gets their first full time job, you should then begin to teach them about basic investment plans. It's never too soon to start saving and investing; and it will help them to learn how to slice up their pay cheque. Teach them about how to make the most of their account package.

THINGS TO AVOID

There are a few things you should avoid doing. Don't allow yourself become the only financial lifeline for your children, young or as adults [2]. If your child overdrafts or overspends, make sure they learn from their mistakes while undergoing little or no harm. If they are damaging their credit, however, you may want to step in and help them out. Don't set their financial goals for them. Let them determine their own goals. It's the only way they'll learn to stay financially disciplined.

In short, the sooner you start teaching your children how to be fiscally responsible the more likely it will become a part of how they manage their finances. Continue to advise them on their finances as they take up a job and begin to think about savings and investment. Yet, don't exert too much control over their decisions; remain an adviser, not a manupulator. We are to go all the way through this journey with our kids and are to get them through the more difficult aspects of it.

Pete had a son who had just got his first job, and though he didn't need it, Pete requested that his son pay him 25% of his wages. He explained how this would be what he would pay in rent if he were to be earning his money in the real-world, where bills and rent are commonplace. In doing so, Pete ensured that he didn't become a financial lifeline to his son, as he now knew the value of money and knew more about budgeting than he would ever have done otherwise. Pete did put this money into a trust for his son, so everybody was a winner.

LET THEM DECIDE

Now that you have begun the process, and are working to change the model your kids have lived by, get rid of allowances; determine the appropriate amount for them to manage, and help them work out a spending plan. You need to let them manage what's available to them. This is key to their success. If you continue to intervene when you think, or even know, they are making a mistake, they would have a diminished opportunity to learn.

You will need to take a position of an adviser and counsellor. What I mean is, it is okay for you to give them advice on a spending decision, and it is perfectly acceptable to try to help them work through all the benefits and detriments to a decision. The hard part is leaving the final decision to them.

Of course, there will be times you may have to step in and say enough is enough, or I am sorry, but you can't do that because X, Y or Z.

I know of a couple whose child had made some very questionable decisions regarding the spending of her money. Rather than taking care of the mobile/cellphone bill, car insurance and maintenance, school expenses, and other agreed responsibilities, this child chose to spend virtually all of her money on clothes, App Store downloads, entertainment, and eating out. When the parents terminated the mobile phone contract and confiscated the car keys from her because it was uninsured, their child couldn't understand why, and thought her parents were being so unreasonable.

As parents, it's obviously very difficult to tell your child something they don't want to hear - especially if it's something you don't want to even acknowledge yourself. But, think "Enough is enough." Intervene when the mistake isn't going to be learnt from otherwise, as the consequences otherwise may be critical.

In time, the child did realise her mistakes and now has a much healthier relationship with money, now prioritising the importance of keeping her car on the road and having a working phone, over clothes she doesn't really need.

I believe the parents did the right thing in this case.

First, there was the basic responsibility of the child paying for the benefit of the mobile/cellphone use. It would have been a different situation if the parents had agreed to pay the phone bill; but that was not the agreed conditions. The second, and more important responsibility, was the uninsured driver and responsibility to others. If this teen had caused an accident while the car was not insured, the injured persons and their damaged property would not be indemnified, being with no insurance cover. Then the parents would have had to pay for the injuries and damages.

With most children, once they realise there is a limited supply of income and they are in control of where it goes, they begin to get very interested in prioritising the things they want to spend their money on and getting the best deal they can. This is where they begin to learn the difference between "cheap" and a "goodbuy". Help them discern when a good deal really is a good deal, versus a "cheap" but bad deal.

A VITAL QUESTION

Help your child to stay focused on the spending plan they set up. Teach them to ask the question advertisers don't want asked: "Is it in my spending plan?" Asking this question alone is a very powerful tool for bringing control and checks to spending. It tends to force you to think about why you are buying an item. In other words, is it a priority? If it is not, don't buy it. Save your money for something of greater value to you [3]. Kids must know how not to spend money on things they can do without.

Watch how your child responds to that question. Yet, if it's not in their spending plan, it's still OK if they go ahead and make the purchase, as long as they have figured out how to adjust the spending plan to include it, and as long as they have not compromised their obligations to other categories for which they have responsibilities. If they buy it and have not figured out how to fit it into their spending plan, it is only a matter of time before the plan falls apart.

I want to mention that, in the case just described, of the child not properly managing her income, the parents did not employ any of these steps until the teen was sixteen and working a part-time job. Prior to this point, the teen had been given an allowance, and pretty much whatever spending money she asked for.

When the child got a typical part-time job, the parents began to try to implement a plan similar to what I am building up here. Most teens have no prior experience dealing with these kinds of decisions and hardly want to start. They expect their parents to bail them out and are not only surprised when the demand is placed on them, but become angry when it doesn't happen.

HOARDING ISN'T RIGHT

A cautionary note regarding children managing money: Some kids will tend to hoard their money. You will need to remind them that money is a tool to help us make our way through life, and it's a very good thing to save up; but it is not good to hoard money. Spending is just as important as saving, as it's not a realistic idea to hoard your finances, as most often through life this won't be achievable.

A tool that is not used is of no value. Money is a tool to purse. Money is the instrument that helps us accomplish our purpose or assignment. Money is like a spoon, a tool that you use to eat food so your body is healthy; so you want to get the tool. Spoon is not the main thing, it is a tool. The same with education; it is a tool to help render products and services better, to develop the mind etc.

In the same vein, money is a vehicle or tool. If money is not serving as a tool to help fulfil assignments, then, rather than serve a useful purpose, it becomes harmful, as it eventually enslaves and destroys those who have it.

To minimise the potential for hoarding money, be sure when you set up a spending plan with your child that there are things that have to be purchased by them. As stated in my earlier book, 101 *Tips for Child Development*, give them just enough to force them to have to choose. This will help to reduce the hoarding tendency. One of the indicators that they are hoarding is if they are inclined to shift spending onto others, like you or another sibling or friend.

I have seen families that have one child that spends money on anything and everything in an effort to be liked, or simply because they like to spend money; and a second child with a hoarding bent. The hoarder will gladly let the spendthrift pay for everything while the hoarder stockpiles money. A well designed spending plan helps to control both of these extremes.

AVOIDING DEBT

Debt is something everybody should want to avoid [4]. An extremely important note to therefore consider is: Teach your children that if they don't spend more than they have, they will never be in debt. This can start at surprisingly young ages. Even if you have sat down with your children and have helped them to put together a really good spending plan, there is always the temptation to spend tomorrow's income today. For kids, guess who the bank is. Very likely it is you. Be aware, if you have refused to be the financier of their allowances, they will often hit relatives and friends up for this "cash advance".

Getting into debt is pretty easy, getting out is where the

challenge is; it's never easy. My husband and I work with several young people and families to help them get back on track. As your child learns the ropes of managing their income, they will gain confidence and increased self-esteem. You will be equipping them for a greater chance of being successful as adults.

Georgina asked her parents about Christmas presents. She asked why her best friend Tarni received £500 worth of Christmas presents last year but she didn't even receive half of what Tarni got. Georgina was confused because Tarni's mum didn't work, but both Georgina's parents did. Georgina wondered how Tarni's mum could afford it.

Georgina's parents then had to explain the financial situation of Tarni's mum - somebody who was frivolous with her spending and over Christmas would typically spend more than she had, just to make sure her child had plenty of presents.

In explaining the situation thoroughly, Georgina's parents were able to reinforce just how important it is to only spend what you have, rather than getting into debt over trivial things. Georgina then understood how Tarni's mum was careless with her spending, and that's the only reason why she got more than her for Christmas.

2

TEACHING KIDS FINANCIAL MANAGEMENT

If it ever bothered your mind that cramming so much into the brain of a child about finances will be over tasking their psychomotor unnecessarily, then I need to tell you not to underestimate their capacity either. Kids begin to learn from the things they interact with from quite early in life.

I can assure you that children come to know about money from very early in life. With their little fingers they point at the things they like when they stroll the aisles with you at the shopping mall. They see you pick up a product and pay for it at the checkout. In their subconscious they know that money is exchanged for goods we need. So talking about money with kids is not over labouring their brains at all.

You can start at any age, but starting between four and six

years old is the ideal age for most kids. At that age, kids are old enough to understand, but not too old to be unyielding.

GOOD OUTLOOK TO LIFE

If your child's worldview is internally centred and focused on their immediate gratification, that child will grow up tending to associate their worth to what they do or don't have. As they have more money and things, they will tend to feel more secure and better about their circumstances. Conversely, they will feel less secure, more anxious, and under greater stress as their income and savings decrease.

Your children's worth is not related to what they have; it's about who they are. As they change their focus from an internal view to the world outside and long range plans and goals, they will begin to feel better about themselves and the world around them. One way to do this is to find a Charity that helps kids of their age group. You may also get someone they can relate to, which makes it real.

There are many good choices, both locally and internationally. It does not have to be a donation of money. In fact, it is best if it is the use of their time and abilities. Most communities have outreach services to the homeless, the less fortunate and infirm. With most children, once they see how well off they have in comparison to others, not only will they want to help out with their time and energy, but will also desire to help out financially.

USING MONEY WELL

Money is a tool to be used. There is nothing magical about it; it doesn't have great powers nor is it more special than any other tool. It has a specific purpose, and when used within the bounds of that purpose, money can be very effective in making our lives less stressful.

Money is a way devised over time to help us keep track of transactions. Sometimes the transaction is our time and effort exchanged for purchasing power (money). Other times it is for tracking the actual purchase of goods or services. Its power, like any other tool, is derived from the person using it. Like a hammer or pair of pliers, money can be used for our benefit or detriment. It all depends on our attitudes, abilities, and intents.

As a parent, a key responsibility of yours is to help your children learn the benefits and drawbacks associated with money. If you can help them to learn that money comes from invested effort and wise decisions, they will begin to appreciate money for what it is, as a tool that is itself "bought" with their energy, time and talents.

Helping children to learn how to maximise their time by

choosing wisely when making that exchange can go a long way to improving their confidence, self-esteem and sense of wellbeing. If wise decisions are not made, one becomes overwhelmed and out of control with foreboding anxiety.

MONEY MUST BE EARNED

When your children think that your finances are endless, they will happily spend every single penny you have - and still ask for more when you're done. They will learn to cajole you, pester you, threaten you, publicly embarrass you, and do whatever else they can to get you to part with your hard earned cash to get what they want. Imagine the four-year-old who went shopping with his mum at the mall yelling for something he wants at whatever cost.

You will therefore need to teach your kids that money comes from hard work, perseverance, skill and talent [5] - and that a combination of those qualities will give them their best chance of success. Work is what you create. Work is a pleasure, not punishment. There is pleasure beholding your work of creation. Work is calling purpose to be fulfilled, and it's something that satisfies you. Such delightful work is whatever you get satisfaction from doing.

When you work you make things happen, and derive great pleasure from that, not just the money you earn doing your work; the money does not matter to you as much as the pleasure you derive from what you do. Kids must be encouraged to derive pleasure from work and learn to serve freely. As they do so freely, they discover their skills and develop the skills so that they are in demand. They can then go to university to add value to the discovered skill and bring it to the best level.

THE HELEN'S STORY

Helen had been a caring person from four years old. She had always wanted to be a nurse; she plays nurse and doctor games and consciously watches YouTube videos on her interest to improve herself continually as a nurse. She spends all her time, reading, and helping people; because, for her, it is a passion, for she found her purpose for existence on time. She never did any of her services for money. She always wanted to please God with the gift she has, and care so much for the people, especially the sick, and thinks about how best to care for them.

By this disposition, Helen was able to set herself free from work that makes others to labour just because they need the money. She discovered her passion and found how she could add value to herself. She developed her skills and made herself so valuable that she became highly in demand because she was able to offer quality care service to others.

Helen's passion and calling corresponded with her skills. She worked for the government hospital for a while to develop herself enough; then after five years she started her own practice. She was able to work at her own pace and to obey the dictates of her conscience. She was happy because she started working for her passion. Many people are not so happy because what they are doing is not their passion. Helen's passion was what gave her money; it was her hobby, and she became master of money.

She was able to save some money for three years before taking the next step of investing in her own practice. Thereafter, she stopped working for money, but sends money to work for her, thus becoming master over money. Money ceased to command her to go to work, thereby depriving her of holidays for those three years. Now, she can take her holiday anytime she likes because she has mastered money.

MASTER OVER MONEY

Only those with too much money, or those that don't need money as they have no outgoings, can be the masters of their finances. When you don't have to work because there is need to earn money, only then are you a master over money; only then is money your tool. Or, when you have too much money and that you don't even know what you'd spend it all on. When you use £10 to get petrol for your car or to do other stuff, these are the times when the power you have over your finances can be diminished.

If you truly are a master of your finances, you may wish to spend £100 in an investment to yield for a couple of years of interest, in return to do what your passion is. Without money to pursue your passion, a couple of things could be hard.

There are times when things are not within your control, and may not always work out perfectly. However, if you can begin to help your child grasp the concept of what money is, where it comes from, and how to get it, they will be better prepared for those times when things don't go as planned.

Directly connected to their view of money is how they get it. If you simply dole it out as allowances or in other unearned ways, they would come to expect it from you. Associate their income to assigned responsibilities as part of the family. The starting point for this step is figuring out how much you are already spending on them. Based on their age, abilities, and how far along they are on the path of financial progress. Specifically attach a portion of that amount directly to these assigned responsibilities.

Sit down with them and work through a spending plan for their income. The minimum categories should be Savings, General Expenses, and Charitable Giving. As your child matures in this area, re-evaluate their plan and help them make adjustments.

TIPS FOR CONTROLLING MONEY

The following tips will help you train your child to have mastery over money:

1. Allow Them to Manage Money:

After you and your child have established the source of their income, give them the responsibility of managing it [6]. This can only be done after they have received an education in personal finance. Yes, they will make mistakes, but it's important to let them. It's far better that they do this now, than later in life when those mistakes really count, and can be disastrous.

2. You Must Be Able to Say No:

Saying "No" to bailing your child out of particular financial situations can be one of the more difficult steps for training him or her on financial mastery. It is related to the previous step of letting them manage money by themselves. If you can't say no, they won't learn what you teach them, and will be unable to resist that impulse purchase that can wreak havoc on their spending plan. Keeping finances away from children can make lead them down a path to more frivolous spending when they are old enough to earn their own money and then have the opportunity to spend it.

3. Savings Will Save Them from Disaster:

When money is handed to a child, they must already be knowledgeable of the importance of self-finances, in order to control the instinct, appetite and taste for spending; and this will make kids wealthy inside. Children must:

- Overcome the materialism that comes with money, and the modern day pressures of consumerism.
- Overcome the power of instinct before becoming grown up.

Saving will help them learn to control the pressure to buy what they don't need. It will control the push of money which makes people not to have money.

Especially in society today, where social media is very accessible and more popular than ever before, children are becoming more materialistic. Impulse purchasing is more frequent than ever before in this digital age, and buying things on a whim for 'likes', 'comments' and 'follows' is commonplace. Savings may just save them from any disasters that may have otherwise been caused by this. Just ensure they have a clear understanding of why we keep savings for emergencies and important life events.

JOE'S EXAMPLE

Joe wanted to buy a toy for £5 when he visited the White Rose Shopping Centre, Leeds, with his mum. He had his savings of five pounds but wanted his mum to use her money to buy it. Although he asked his mum nicely, she replied, "A toy does not cost much, just five pounds; but a million pounds is lots of five pounds put together in the same savings pot." He requested to use the money from his wallet instead, but mum advised otherwise, reinforcing her point about saving where you can afford to.

Everything small becomes big, if you keep it up for long enough. Spending £5 per week doesn't sound like much, but that's £260 across the year. That is the point Joe's mum wished to make. Everything adds up. When you continue to save what you have, you will have bigger money in a matter of time. When it is big enough, you can then invest it, and the returns you get from that investment can be used to buy the toy. Hence you retain your initial saving. When you can manage small things, they become big. If you save five pounds a month, that will make thousands of money in 10 years. No amount of money is too small to save or invest. As we saw earlier, even £5 a week can soon add up to a sizeable sum.

Saving a small sum every now and then will not make you

rich, but saving consistency, regularly and over a long period of time, will. Most things we buy for our children are not necessary; the money can be saved. Kids must love us not based on gifts, but on life values that we imparted in them while they are in our care.

Saving serves two purposes for most young kids. First, it is used for a planned "big ticket" item such as a nice toy, bicycle or car. The second purpose is for the unplanned events and expenses they encounter. Without both parts, the spending plan is pretty much doomed to failure and frustration.

4. Giving It Away Will Help Them Grow:

Use charitable giving of both their time and income to teach children there is a much bigger world out there, and they have the ability to make a difference. Teach them the invaluable attitude of "I can make a difference." Give them the power to make a difference with money, promote healthy spending, saving and giving.

5. It's OK to Talk about Money:

It's okay to talk about money [7]. Include your children in some of the family's money decisions. Keep it simple, and base it on their ability to understand it. It's not necessary to show them your pay stubs. Give them the bank statements or the family spending plan. Just give them a chance to have input on some basic spending decisions.

6. Tell Them about Your Choices:

Tell your children about some money mistakes you made. Maybe it was a "Get-Rich-Quick" plan that didn't work out so well. Tell them about some of the things you got right, like refinancing the mortgage so you can get it paid off earlier and save several thousands of pounds or dollars. They will appreciate the trust you have shown them.

SEE JUDE AND JACK

Jude told his son Jack about Forex trading which his friend introduced him to, and how he found out by his experience that it was not a good business for him. He said he will not advise his son to go into it as he now sees it as gambling, and the easiest way to lose money. "Don't be in a hurry to make money; you will lose money that way," he told Jack.

People who want to defraud you know you want to make money quick. For example, MLM and forex are not for money making, nor is network marketing a good way to make money either, as only those at the top of the pecking order make the money. Save consistently and discipline your desires. It is not how much you save but how much you spend.

7. Teach Them about Compounded Interest:

The "magic" of compounded interest can help your children achieve their goals much sooner, just as the reverse can bury their goals in financial bondage. At their young age, this is generally not an issue, but if they can learn it now, it could make a big difference in their future.

8. Don't Give Up, and Don't Give In:

No matter what tactics your children might use to wear you down, it is important for you to stand strong. Kids can really take their toll on your mental and physical wellbeing if you let them, but if you don't give in, eventually they will understand they are wasting their time and energy, and find that life is much better using a different approach.

JOHN AND JACK

John, 49, from Wakefield, was falling victim to the wide-eyed requests of his grandson, Jack. Jack, who John wished to please (as it was his first grandchild and sought his affection at every given moment), would always give in after the third or fourth plea for a new toy in the shop.

"Please granddad John, I really like Ben 10" he would say, over and over again. Wide-eyed, knowing his Granddad would eventually cave, Jack knew exactly how to play the situation.

John unfortunately couldn't stand strong, until his daughter (Jack's mother) imparted her wisdom on him. She informed him that the only reason he does it is because he knows his granddad will cave and buy him the toy. So, John's daughter told him to stand strong and don't give in, saying "He will soon realise he's wasting his time and energy and he'll give up."

3

LEARN TO SAY NO

Let's start with an example. Your child is saving to pay the fee to play a sports game, and then decides to spend the savings on the latest games console game. It's OK for you to remind the child that they are saving up so they can play sports. Then help them to come to the conclusion that by making the choice to buy the game, they will not have enough to play the sport. It is better if they can think through this on their own with some coaching from you. If you tell them they can't immediately have the video game, it will not have the same impact; and they are less likely to own the decision.

It's okay to say no every now and then [8]. You are not the bad guy for doing so.

If they choose to spend the money on that game, you need to let them. Of course this will depend on the age and ability of the child. For younger children, I would not make a sport's fee a part of their income.

When it comes time for the sport's fee and they don't have the funds to cover it, you will need to let them not play the sport for that season.

Yes, as a parent, it will be tough to allow your child to bear the result of their decisions, and may even be an additional burden on you. But they will learn several very powerful lessons. They will discover that money is limited in its supply; that all choices we make have trade-offs; and they are responsible to manage the decisions they make.

If you choose to bail them out, you will be teaching them equally powerful lessons. You will be teaching them that you really don't mean what you say. They will begin to view your words more as a suggestion than meaning what you say. You will be teaching them that they don't have to be responsible for their choices. You will be teaching them that as long as someone else has money, they will get bailed out. And you will be demonstrating to them that our choices don't really matter because someone else will cover for us.

Having a good, solid spending plan will give your children a guide for making spending decisions. It will help them to make informed decisions and to prioritise what's important to them. It will teach them that impulse purchases have effects beyond the moment.

Your kids need to learn to say "No" as well. When faced with that impulse purchase or opportunity, they need to ask the question, "Is it in my spending plan?" If it is not, then don't buy it. If they still want it, you need to let them make that decision. But, with that decision they should be able to demonstrate to you how they are going to work it into the spending plan. If they can't, it is still their decision and you need to let them learn the hard lesson of not participating in that sport they traded it for.

If they really do want it, I believe having them figure out how they will work it into their spending plan is the better approach. First, have them wait for three days before making the decision to buy. If they still want it, have them make the appropriate changes to their spending plan and begin to set aside a portion of their income into the savings category until they save up enough to buy the game for their console.

MORE WORK FOR MONEY

Another option is for them to try to figure out how to come up with the additional needed money. This may mean taking on additional jobs around the house, or maybe in the neighbourhood. Here in the UK, this isn't quite as common, but is certainly worth a try if you have elderly neighbours who may need a hand every now and then. If your child chooses to do jobs around the house, don't make it too easy on them to achieve their goal.

Your child will learn that if it is worth having, it is worth the wait and work invested. The time invested will make the reward so much sweeter. They will learn the value of saving for the future. In many instances, they will decide after a time that the Xbox game wasn't such a great idea after all, and end up not buying it. The lesson here is that impulse purchases can be far more costly than the purchase price. In this example, the opportunity of playing sports was nearly lost to a fleeting whim to have that game.

Remember, a spending plan is basically a priority list. If your child deciding to have that new game is more important than playing sports, then so be it. Of course there will be times when you have to step in and stop the transaction. But these should be the rare exceptions.

One of the most important things we can get them to learn

is to ask the question, "Is this purchase something I have allowed for in my spending plan?" If the answer is "No", then don't buy it. If you can teach your children this concept, they will be well on their way to a less stressful adult life.

It may seem to you that I have not given adequate attention to this step. It is just that simple. If you and your child have followed the guidance so far, then you have answered the How-much-is-enough question, and built a spending plan. By doing this, you have said this is how much we have to work with, and these are the priorities.

Plans and priorities change, but any of these changes should be based on well thoughtout goals and not on an impulsive reaction. Learning to say "No" to these impulses will keep you and your child on the path of progress.

LUCY AND LAYNE

Lucy, 32, from Newcastle, reinforced the points above with her daughter Layne from a very young age. She taught the importance of understanding the word 'no' and why you shouldn't reroute your life over potentially-pointless purchases.

"Learning self-control is important" Lucy explained.

"That's why I have a spending plan, here, take a look" she continued.

Lucy proceeded to show Layne her detailed spending plan that she kept on her smartphone, and the importance of staying on-route with your finances, instead of allowing impulse purchases to take control. Layne learnt all about spending plans from a very young age and will therefore be wiser with her spending habits as she becomes old enough to manage her own finances.

4

MONEY AND KIDS

Money isn't scarce, at least in the mind of a child. Children have endless amounts of purchasing power (in billions, even if in their minds only), resources they believe are available to them directly or indirectly. Yet, they are rarely taught about money, or more importantly, the management of money. Some parents are as guilty as the next parent on making it a point to teach their kids about money and money management skills.

THE MYSTERY OF MONEY

Of course, the generation gap combined with the technology age in which kids now live has a big part in lack of focus on this subject. But no more. If for no other reason, you should think for a moment how money is so rapidly transferred today, with just the swipe of a card. And in fact, many people (parents) today hardly ever come in contact with actual paper money anymore.

It's so easy to load up your shopping basket with just the swipe of a card; but there lies the trouble for kids and managing their money today. It's just too easy and there's no immediate pain of actually taking those hard earned pounds/dollars out of your little purse or wallet and parting with your money at the time of the purchase.

First, don't put off teaching your kids about money, the value of it, and how to manage it. It's never too early, in our day and time. When you first begin to acquaint your child with money, be prepared for mistakes and some growing pains understanding the concept of money. It is far better to allow your children to learn from mistakes involving small amounts rather than later in life when the same mistakes can prove financially disastrous. Many financial experts agree that a big mistake is for parents not to allow their children to have control over their money early on.

TEACHING MONEY VALUE

As with teaching children about any subject matter, there

are general guidelines about the level of complexity that is introduced at any particular age; teaching your kids about money management is certainly no exception [9]. So, let's take a look at some general teaching guidelines pertaining to money management and at what age level.

Even with toddlers and preschoolers you can give your child an allowance. Now keep in mind that they will probably play with it, misplace it, and maybe even lose it; but that's perfectly fine. At this age, it is merely introducing the concept that their little bit of money has value and should be kept safe so it will be around when they want to use it.

With the ease and power given to today's consumer, it is difficult to get adults to understand and have the discipline to save for something they want or need to purchase. But even at an age as early as about first year/grade you should begin to take on this challenge with your child — so much of today is instant gratification. And no philosophy will be tougher for you to overcome with your children and money management as this. Delayed gratification or saving for something they want is a very difficult concept to teach kids, and for kids to master; but it is one of the most important things to do to enable them manage their money.

Be sure to continue on with working with your children the delayed gratification concept. In other words, teach them the principle of working and saving for something that they want to get. You'll find (and they will too) that as they learn this lesson, whatever it is they worked, waited and saved for will have much greater value to them personally.

Be sure to check out various online tools and games that can help with teaching the value of money.

BETWEEN NEED AND WANT

The next level you'll want to discuss with and teach your kids are the difference between 'need' and 'want'. This is ever so important today in this media, marketing and consumption society in which we live and our kids are hammered with daily. You won't have to look far for examples of needs versus wants. Just turn on the TV and wait for an advertisement, and now it doesn't even need to be this way. Your child can pick up a tablet or smartphone and each and every application, social media platform and website will display some form of advertising – some of which they are bound to be interested in.

Talk with your kids and discuss what it is the advertisement is going after them for, and why. This is a considerable money management accomplishment for kids when they begin to honestly differentiate between needs and wants.

It's also at this point (early to mid-grade school) that your kids begin to establish some sort of savings plan for something they would like to have (notice I didn't use 'want'). The whole process of budgeting and saving for something at this age will give your kids a great sense of accomplishment, pride, and a first start toward financial confidence. Also at this age, with your kids introduced to saving and budgeting, it is a good time to introduce them to paying for some of the extras that they would like to have for school, sports, band, etc, and for beginning charitable contribution.

From here continue increasing your kid's understanding of budgeting and managing their money by weaning them off from you providing the lion's share of their 'wants', to them working, budgeting, and saving. Simply increase their financial responsibility to them; keep increasing their social responsibility too by giving to charities of yours and their choice.

GROWING INTO FINANCIAL FREEDOM

As your kids progress to their teen years and become more mature, the time will come that you may want to consider getting your child some form of debit card. By this time in their life they'll be considering university or some career path that will quite possibly require some sort of financial allowances/student loan, and at the very least they will be needing even more financial freedom.

A prepaid parent-monitored debit card is an initial good solution. By now, and through these many years of your tutelage, your child has become financially literate and it's all because you started early on teaching your child solid money management skills and attitude.

Do you know you can bring to your kid's knowledge that they too can start earning money for themselves? Never make them believe that without you around them they can't achieve anything. While they grow, each of them has unique trait that makes one different from the other. So, the moment you identify that, let them use that to keep themselves busy, while at the same time making money out of such a service.

A MOTIVATED PHOTOGRAPHER

Emily walked up to her mum one sunny afternoon, requesting that she gets enrolled for a photography class. She was attentive in class, and in no time graduated in flying colours. That skill would have deteriorated were it not for her father's intervention, having invited her for a photo session at his place of work. The end of the year's party was so thrilling that after the party, Emily was appreciated and given stipends. She was highly commended for her creativity during the event. Since then, she had taken that serious to the extent that in her school, she, most times, feature as the school's photographer.

Beyond making resources from what started so little in her father's office, Emily took some shots about nature which people appreciated and paid for. All these she did during her holidays.

As parents, invest in your children's creativity and allow them to make out resources from that. With that, they won't just be financially free; they'll also enjoy what they do passionately. Your children's interests may be found in making of hair, tutoring, coffee shops or carwash, social media influencer, Paper boy or newspaper rounds, helping at the corner shops to distribute newspapers to the old people in the morning before they go to school, which will fetch them a couple of coins/notes at the end of the week. This will go a far-reaching way in decreasing the rate at which they will see you as their lifeline. Also, they'll see themselves as being responsible more than others.

All they will ever need in life is whatever it is that will make them feel free to express themselves. Hence, if they are accountable for the choices they make, they'd see more reasons to do what they needed to do well at the appropriate time.

A LIST OF POSSIBILITIES

There are countless possibilities of money earning activities kids at different ages can engage their creativities in this modern age. My list here is not exhaustive.

1. Event planning for their own programmes
2. Headgear tie for events
3. YouTube uploads
4. Blogging
5. Social media influencer
6. Logo design
7. Game design and development
8. Graphic design
9. Poster and Flyer design and distribution
10. Banner ad
11. Photoshop editing
12. T-shirt design and presentation
13. Modelling
14. Music
15. Web traffic
16. Translating and interpreting other languages
17. Animation for kids

18. Comics Producer and composer
19. Video editing
20. Viral video
21. Making of greeting cards
22. Data entry
23. Mobile app

Depending on their age and exposure, kids get to take pleasure in some of these activities anyway, and earning money doing any of these is added fun.

GREGG

Gregg was a talented artist and had a love for fashion. At the young age of 14, he had already designed his own t-shirt. Though, he was doing this solely for his own personal benefit, giving him something unique.

His father, however, insisted that he learn the value of money and put his entrepreneurial skills to work, challenging him to turn his talent into a viable business. He promised that there would be a 'reward' for his efforts by the end.

Little did Gregg know; the reward would be the money he would make from his school friends after the t-shirt business was successful. His father pushed him to utilise his 'possibility' and make his own money, and that's exactly what Gregg did.

Not only did this teach Gregg valuable skills in terms of personal finance, but it strengthened his entrepreneurial skills, toughened him to the real-world of earning money and prepared him for later life.

5

SAVINGS

Everyone has the opportunity to do something with their money; some squander money and soon fall under its control, while those who master money save and invest it till when it can serve a better use.

THE COMING RAINY DAY

Savings will save your child from a future financial disaster. For kids, there are generally two reasons for saving money. One reason is to save up for a specific purchase, like a toy, a bicycle, a game system, a car or university. The second reason is to be prepared for unexpected purchases [10]. Mastering how to save will help to convert a spending plan disaster to a simple decision.

The first reason: saving for a particular "big ticket" item, should be built into the spending plan. The money is set aside for a specific purpose — this is teaching your child long range planning. Using the comparison shopping skills you have taught them, they would decide how much they will need to make this purchase. Then using the spending plan, they are able to figure out how much they need to save out of each income source to get to that goal in a given time frame.

A cautionary note: As mentioned in the chapter on learning to say no, impulse buying can delay or even derail this part of the plan. When your child sees something they want right now, and then remembers they have this money saved up, they will be tempted to act on impulse and spend the savings for a purchase that the money was not intended for. This is where you will need to remind them of their goal and the purpose of the money.

An essential tactic to reduce this impulse, is to have that money stashed away in a bank account or a place that is not easily accessed. Many people choose to invest their money in ISA accounts and premium bonds. These cannot easily be accessed but are there when/if you really need them – allowing you to keep a decent sum behind you, whilst earning interest. In terms of premium bonds, you also have the chance to win monthly sums of money too.

Your children should not have the money on them. Unless

they are ready to make the purchase for which the money was intended, it needs to be tucked away safely.

Do not be their "Ready Cash" or "Pay Day Loan" machine. What I mean by this is, you will most likely be asked, or you may even feel like you want to "help" them out and "loan" them the money until you get home. Avoid this impulse. You want them to learn how to resist this type of buying and to learn how to make the wiser purchases.

The second reason for saving money is to be prepared for those unforeseen expenses. For example, it may be that unplanned trip to the water park with a friend or the above mentioned impulse purchase. For an older child it might be they lost their mobile/cell phone and want to replace it. Again, you would not want your child to have this money on them. If it is in their pockets, they are far more likely to spend it on something other than intended. It should be tucked away safely. This enforces a waiting period, which helps to reduce poor purchasing decisions.

WHY HOARDING HURTS

Another caution: Some kids tend to hoard their money unnecessarily. Though this sounds like it could only be a positive thing, in fact, it can unfortunately be as bad as not having any kind of spending plan at all. Hoarding has a tendency to lead to an attitude of arrogance. As they pile up more and more money, they will start to feel they are better than others.

Another danger in hoarding is the anxiety it can cause. As your child builds up this cash pile, they begin to attach their worth to it, and feel happier about it as it grows; and when it comes time to spend it, as the pile of money goes down, they could become more and more anxious. The amount of money stocked up becomes the barometer for their mood. As the amount increases, so does their sense of security; as it decreases, they become anxious, moody, feeling insecure.

To keep your kids feeling like they don't have as much, they will resist spending it, and even try to find ways to transfer their expenses to others. Having a good, solid spending plan helps to alleviate this improper response to money.

MORE THAN MONEY

Good as money is, it must not be your primary source of joy and happiness. If anything is giving you joy other than true love of God, then that thing will spoil in your hand. Having Love should be your primary source of joy and happiness, not money. Kids must be free from making physical things to determine their source of joy and happiness. Our real wealth is knowing true love of God, but people gravitate towards physical things that are visible to identify.

Some kids work for money because they want to have a better identity, looking at how much money they are worth and how much physical things they have. This is why they want to increase the physical things they have. This attitude encourages pride.

Kim always daydreams about how much money would be given to her by her rich uncle. But when the uncle finally arrives and gives her a fiver, she gets so disappointed because she had daydreamed on getting £100, just because the uncle is rich. She had looked forward to pleasure herself on what she wanted to buy.

Kim was disappointed and felt unhappy because she let her joy to depend on the money she expected from someone. She ought to know that rich people tend to be very frugal with their money because they worked hard for it. She ought to have asked her uncle to give her an opportunity to use her skills and work in his establishment both to improve her skills and earn something for self. It is the sort of request rich people like to respond to.

It is the sort of thing that adds value to oneself and makes one rich inside, thereby increasing one's worth. It makes one to be valued by others, and it always pays better than largesse doled out by benevolent people.

BOB

Bob had a somewhat unpleasant experience in his life, in which he bumped into somebody he went to school with, some twenty years ago. Fred, his childhood friend, was only speaking about the things he had bought, like his brand-new Range Rover, his six-bedroom house and his newly-designed cinema room.

As good as money can be for somebody, Bob knew that Fred's primary source of happiness was his substantial bank balance and the things he could therefore afford to buy. In seeing how Fred talked about money, Bob acknowledged and knew all the reasons why he should never fall into that trap.

Bob's happiness came from his family, and that was only reinforced due to his interaction with Fred – who was very materialistic and was relying on money and belongings to fill certain emotional voids in his life.

6

BUILDING A SPENDING PLAN

What if I titled this Chapter, "Money Costs Money"? It would explain my intention here, wouldn't it? Because your child's financial training is like going on a long trip without a map. You might get there eventually, but the number of unintended detours, backtracking and wrong turns along the way will cost you in time and money.

There's also the frustration and insecurity of not knowing if you are in a safe place or even if you are travelling in the right direction. It is only a well-designed spending plan, like a good map, that will make the journey go a lot smoother.

SPENDING MAP FOR CHILDREN

Having a spending plan teaches your child the value of saving for "big ticket" items – that special toy they really want, a gift for a family member, fees for their sports clubs and social activities with their friends, for example – while at the same time managing the day-to-day expenses – a chocolate bar at the checkout line, a drink and a burger at the local football game, or App Store download. It reinforces and helps them to learn priority-setting.

There are few things in life that reflect a person's priorities more than how they spend their money. To paraphrase what I once heard someone say, "Let me see how you spend your money and take a look at what you throw away, and I can tell a lot about what is important to you." A spending plan forces us to realise what's important to us.

For younger children, you should help them to set up a very basic spending plan. Have one fund to save for those big ticket items like the bicycle they really want. Have another fund for general spending, the day-to-day items like the chocolate bar at the supermarket checkout or a small toy. Have them set up a third fund for charitable giving. If you have a special Charity you support, let them pitch in.

For example, here is Compassion UK link. https://www.

compassionuk.org/sponsorship/

Involving children makes it more real for them. It is important that our children understand that life exists beyond ourselves, and that sometimes we can be a part of helping someone else in their time of need.

If you are starting this with a younger child, the one thing that works well is to get a three part bank that is labeled for spending, savings, and charity. When pay day comes around, teach them to put at least 10% in the savings bank, 10% in the charity bank, and the remainder in the spending bank. If you are going to have them make the purchases for birthday gifts for friends or family members, have them put more than 10% in the savings portion. Having them buy the gifts is a good idea because it gives them a feeling of happiness and fulfilment if they are directly involved in the giving.

Regardless of where the money comes from, whether it is income from you or a gift from a grandparent, teach them to divide it into the three categories. This will keep them from seeing money as anything other than the tool that it is. If it is given to them for a specific purchase – say, grandma gave them the money as a birthday gift toward the purchase of a new bike – then all of it would be placed in the bank associated with that purchase. In this example, it would all go into the savings bank.

SPENDING MAP FOR TEENS

As your child approaches secondary/high school the categories will be more complex. Many people have talked about having a "Miscellaneous" category. I recommend you avoid it. What we have seen happen over the years is that a lot of things get dumped here when they should belong somewhere more specific. If you feel you must have this category, teach your teen to use it sparingly and watch it closely.

With older children you can do a realistic evaluation of the cost of everything you and your child can think of to meet their basic needs and longterm goals. Include everything you would probably be paying for anyway. Depending on their previous involvement, it is quite likely that your two lists won't match exactly. Don't worry about it, start with everything you both can think of, then work backwards.

Once you have compiled the list, review it in relation to your child's age and ability to grasp the concepts. Decide what they are ready to take on and what you should keep. Don't be afraid to stretch a little; this is how they grow. Because we want to maintain control, most parents do not give their children sufficient responsibility. Resist this urge.

Remember, this should be a "zero-sum" event for you. You should not be giving them any more than what you would have spent on them in the first place. The only real difference is how it gets managed, and by whom. Be prepared for a surprise. You will likely discover that you are buying a lot more than you think.

THE NEED FOR SUPERVISION

In the beginning, keep a close eye on how your child is doing. This is a critical point in the process; it establishes the foundation for their future success. As your child demonstrates an ability to manage and make right decisions you can give over more control. If you began at an early age, by the time they are ready for secondary/high school you will have a pretty good idea of how they will do.

As your child matures it will be necessary to make adjustments: to alter the amount given, the categories, and responsibilities along the way. It is all part of your child learning how responsibility is related to privilege. Strictly from a parenting position, it is easier to increase the money than decrease it, and it is easier to reduce the responsibilities than increase them. Do not let ease and personal comfort overshadow the growing opportunity this experience provides your child.

Of all of the steps, this one is the most important. If your child enters adulthood understanding how to manage what they have, it won't matter as much about their income.

Why? They will know how to be successful with whatever they have. Teach your kids how to build their own map to a more victorious money management plan. When they become adults, they will be far better prepared to meet the challenges that defeat many families everyday.

ZOE

Zoe's mum documented her daughter's financial education journey. Noting any changes that she made to her ability to comprehend the importance of finance, any decisions she was able to make and how her attitude towards money changed. This can be found underneath and comprises of several snippets from the journal.

Age 5 – Taught Zoe that money is not endless.

Age 6 – Began to give Zoe pocket money. Reinforced the importance of saving, and how she can get something 'big' with her money if she doesn't spend it for a long period of time.

Age 9 – Zoe is becoming more materialistic. I continue to reinforce the importance of saving. Little success. Hopefully she learns from her mistakes.

Age 13 – Zoe now has social media. Sponsored posts are giving her wild ideas about what to spend her money on.

7

WAYS TO TEACH KIDS ABOUT MONEY

Teaching Kids could be great fun; that's if you know how. Those who don't easily get frustrated and abandon the business altogether. Let me offer some simple technics for teaching children, especially the very tender ones.

TEACHING PRE-SCHOOLERS AND KINDERGARTNERS ABOUT MONEY

This is the most fun group of kids to teach. Here is how:

1. USE A CLEAR JAR TO SAVE.

The piggybank is a great idea, but it doesn't give kids a visual. When you use a clear jar, they see the money growing. Yesterday, they had a pound/dollar bill and five dimes. Today, they have a pound/dollar bill, five dimes and a quarter! Talk through this with them and make a big deal about it growing!

Every thing small becomes big. When you continue to save what you have you will have bigger money in a matter of time. When it is big enough, you can then invest it, and the returns you get from that investment can be spent; hence you retain your initial saving. When you can manage small things, they become big. If you pay the price of waiting for it to grow, you will get the best. Interestingly, kids this age can understand what the clear jar demonstrates.

2. SET AN EXAMPLE

A study found that money habits in children are formed by the time they're seven years old. They can see your example and will do as you do. So bear in mind always, little eyes are watching you. If you're slapping down plastic every time you go out to dinner or the grocery store, they'll eventually notice. Or if you and your spouse are arguing about money, they'll notice that too. Set a healthy example for them and they'll be much more likely to follow it when they get older.

3. SHOW THEM THAT STUFF COSTS MONEY

You've got to do more than say, "That pack of toy cars costs £5/ $5, son." Help them grab a few pounds/dollars out of their jar, take it with them to the store, and physically hand the money to the cashier. This simple action will have more impact than a five-minute lecture.

TEACHING ELEMENTARY/PRIMARY PUPILS AND SECONDARY/MIDDLE SCHOOLERS ABOUT MONEY

4. SHOW OPPORTUNITY COST

Opportunity cost is just another way of saying, "If you buy this video game, then you won't have the money to buy that pair of shoes." At this age, your kids should be able to weigh decisions and understand the possible outcomes.

5. GIVE COMMISSIONS, NOT ALLOWANCES

Don't give your kids money for breathing. Pay them commissions based on creative chores they do around the house, like taking out the trash, cleaning their room, or mowing the grass.

Dave and his daughter, Rachel Cruze, talked a lot about this system in their book, *Smart Money Smart Kids.* This concept helps your kids understand that money is earned – it's not just given to them.

6. AVOID IMPULSE BUYS

"Mom, I found this cute dress. It's perfect and I love it! Can we buy it, please?"

Does this sound familiar? This age group really knows how to capitalise on the impulse buy – especially when it uses someone else's money.

Instead of giving in, let your child know they can use their hard-earned commission to pay for it. But encourage your child to wait at least a day before they purchase anything over £10 or $10. It will likely still be there tomorrow, and they'll be able to make that money decision with a level head the next day [11].

7. STRESS THE IMPORTANCE OF GIVING

Once they start making a little money, be sure you teach them about giving. They can pick a church, charity or even someone they know who needs a little help. Eventually, they'll see how giving doesn't just affect the people they give to, but the giver as well.

TEACHING TEENAGERS ABOUT MONEY

8. TEACH THEM CONTENTMENT

Your teen probably spends a good chunk of their time staring at a screen as they scroll through social media. And every second they're online, they're seeing the highlight reel of their friends, family and even total strangers! It's the quickest way to bring on the comparison trap.

Contentment starts in the heart. Let your teen know that their Honda (although not the newest car on the block) is still running well enough to get them from point A to point B. And you can still throw a memorable, milestone birthday dinner/celebration without spending a chunk of your savings funding it!

9. GIVE THEM THE RESPONSIBILITY OF A BANK ACCOUNT

By the time your kid is a teenager, you should be able to set them up with a simple bank account if you've been doing some of the above along the way. This takes money management to the next level, and will, hopefully, prepare them for managing a much heftier account when they get older.

10. GET THEM SAVING FOR UNIVERSITY

There's no time like the present to have your teen start saving for university. Do they plan on working a summer job? Perfect! Take a portion of that (or more) and toss it in a university savings account. Your teen will feel like they have skin in the game as they contribute toward their education.

Putting money in the bank does not particularly make it

grow or increase reasonably, but it retains it till it grows to an amount that can be invested. Money in the bank is not for growth, but to make it work for you; and to do that, it must be invested.

Good education is an investment.

LUCAS

Lucas, a 17-year-old boy from southeast London with a passion for graphic design worked at KFC for three consecutive summers because it was close to his house and he was able to save £3,000. The following September, as he went to university, he wanted to grow his graphic design business, so he used £100 to pay for advertising in *Student Union* as a cover artist designer.

In about a week, he received four clients that wanted him to design their song covers. He made £200; and he kept repeating the process and marketing himself on social media. As his clientele grew, his social media following grew. This meant he could decrease his marketing budget because he can market to his clients directly.

With his increased clientele came more earnings, more savings, more investment with greater returns. That's how people become rich. I call it focus thinking, passionate working habit, perseverance and determination to succeed. No one with these qualities go poor.

After a while of working hard, Lucas was able to multiply his initial savings. All of that happening while his friends were still struggling with money because they consumed the amount they had and didn't think of growth and multiplication. On his part, Lucas found a way to make his capital to work for him.

Everyone came to this world with a gift, talent or ability. In his case, Lucas knew he liked to chat with people and wanted to work in an area where his interest could be developed. He did not know his gift or calling specifically yet, though he knew he was somewhat intelligent and had a passion for graphic design. So, he put what he had to good use.

Some kids think they don't have anything, no gifts, no passion, or no money, just because they don't have physical cash. And this is because they have not converted or increased or multiplied their gifts. Kids must use what they have; and by using what they already have, it will increase and bring returns. That's what Lucas did.

Whatever gifts kids have been given is what you are capable to increase or multiply. But you need to prove you are faithful first in the little you already have before you get an increase. If you are not faithful with little then the little you have will be taken away. This is a divine concept (Matthew 25:14-29). The little one has but fails to use is taken away, lest one abuses it, messes it up, throws it away, missuses it, or uses it to endanger oneself. That is why it is safe to take away from you and give to the guy who has proved to be faithful and responsible enough to multiply the little into something worthwhile.

In this scenario, Lucas learnt how to appropriately manage his finances. He used his initial capital to invest in his future, something many will consider to be forward-thinking, with a 'big picture' mindset.

Lucas was unlike his friends, who prefered to keep working than plan for themselves. Lucas would often consider them to be idle, not utilising their talents to the best of their ability, not seizing every opportunity given to them.

See, the common belief is that lazy children work with their hands, but forward-thinking, intelligent children work with their brains. Those who use their brain manage others in the workplace; they hire people who work with their hands and legs. Or, that's how the saying goes, anyway.

More is entrusted to those who have been tested and tried in responsibility, stewardship, frugality and management of money. God expects us to be faithful with money and shrewdness, which is to make the right financial decisions. To be shrewed is to make well informed decisions to get a better result.

Frugality is the ability to be economical with money so that you can save it, multiply it, and cause it to grow. Frugality is how you demonstrate that you have authority over money. You control it so that you don't come under its slavery; it's how you demonstrate that you are master over money, and not the other way around.

HARRY

Harry was just ten years old when he bought his first Go-Pro camera. This cost a lot of money, but it wasn't simply a frivolous purchase, it was an investment.

See, Harry had been saving his pocket money for some years now. Growing up watching gamers/vloggers on YouTube playing Minecraft and Fortnite, he had long since wanted to become a gamer himself. Luckily, Harry was able to see the 'bigger picture' and noticed that if he saved his £5 pocket money each week for at least a year, he would be able to afford a good Go-Pro to start his own channel – and that's exactly what he did.

Harry quickly became popular and his investment in the Go-Pro camera proved to be worthwhile – as it didn't take long for Harry to reach a wide enough audience that he could monetize his videos. In doing so, he was able to make a steady, regular income from a very young age. His forward-thinking, positive and motivated attitude made him over £500 in his first year as a Minecraft/Fortnite YouTuber.

11. TEACH THEM TO STEER CLEAR OF STUDENT LOANS WHERE POSSIBLE

Some people may not have yet realised, but student loans, though can be very helpful, also have their downfalls. Therefore, where it can be achieved (depending on individual circumstances), they should be avoided.

Before your teen even applies to university, you should likely consider it down and have the talk – the "How are we going to pay for university" talk.

Although universities in the UK provide a lot of help and advice via Student Finance England, it's important to first have a 'plan' of sorts on how you want to approach it but do consider the information on the website.

Let your teen know the later-life implications of student loan, and if it can be avoided, such that if student loans aren't an option to fund their education, it will be a great thing.

Talk through all the alternatives out there, like going to community university, apprenticeship, going to an in-state university, working part-time while in school, and applying for scholarships/bursaries and grants as they apply to different countries and universities.

While you're at it, get Tips for #unilife for them. It's a must-have resource to help our university-bound teen prepare for the next big step in their life.

12. TEACH THEM THE DANGER OF CREDIT CARDS

As soon as your kid turns 18, they'll get hounded by credit card offers – especially once they're in university. If you haven't taught them why debt is a bad idea, they'll become yet another credit card victim. Remember, it's up to you to determine the right time you'll teach them these principles. Just remember this, credit cards can be dangerous [12].

13. GET THEM ON A SIMPLE BUDGET

They should learn the importance of making a plan for their money while they're still under your roof.

14. INTRODUCE THEM TO INVESTMENT OPPORTUNITIES

I know what you're thinking. You can barely get your teens to brush their hair – how in the world are they supposed to become investment savvy?

The earlier your child can get started investing, the better. Investment in their skills will be a good start! Introduce your teen to it at an early age, and they'll get a headstart on preparing for their future.

15. HELP THEM FIGURE OUT HOW TO USE THEIR TIME

When you think about it, teenagers have plenty of free time – whether it's half-terms, Easter, Summer or Christmas. If your teen wants some money (and which teen doesn't?), then help them find a job. Better still, help them become an entrepreneur! These days, it's easier than ever for your teen to start up their own business and turn in profit.

Providing a product or service is essentially what business is in its simplest form. How can kids serve people with their time, talent, and expertise? Have them consider ways they can serve the community.

If necessary, they can begin serving people for free to get them to recognise and discover their value to the community. When they add value, they will always immediately become valuable. Once they have proven themselves, looking for problems to solve and improving on their skills, they can set and negotiate a pay. Make sure to balance the time spent on business with their academic, spiritual, social and other aspects of their life.

8

YOUNG KIDS AND MONEY

Unfortunately, handling money is not something we learn at school. Just like many other life skills that we find necessary in adulthood, money management is also neglected while lots of energy is spent on secondary/high levels of math.

If you examine the curriculum your kids are covering from prep to Year 13, you can understand why many of them will go to university or get tertiary education, but only one kid per class will be upscale. (Though somes schools in the UK have now started to offer Financial literacy alongside maths) Are you ready to make sure it is your kid?

Handling money is something we all need an awareness and knowledge of, long before we leave the family home. When friends have brand-name shoes or a computer game and your kid wants them too, your kid's ability to understand money is going to be very handy. So, if you wonder when it is the right time to learn about money. My answer is: the minute your kid can count to 10.

LEARNING FROM ANTS

Sam's countenance spoke worry when he approached his Maths teacher, after the bi-weekly lesson. He wondered as he drew closer to Steve. *How could an ant prepare their food in the summer? How could we humans that can easily trample ants under the sole of one's feet now go and learn from an ant?* All these ran through his mind. He was oblivious of the fact that Steve observed he was not the usual Sam – lively and energetic after every lesson – he used to know.

"Sam!" The teacher called out to him.

"Yes, sir!" Sam replied timidly as he continually rubbed his eyes with the back of his hand while he walked wobbly towards the direction of the teacher.

"You look worried. Hope all is well with you?"

"Not at all. I've been thinking about your lesson this morning, and I seem a little bit confused!" Sam let out the words gently as he looked into the eyes of the teacher. That provoked laughter out of the teacher's mouth.

"Let's take a walk around this place a bit. Do you have some minutes to spare?"

"And my parents?"

"I'll walk you home for them to be rest assured that you've been with me," he assured Sam as they walked at arm's length.

As both of them walked to the school's playground in silence, Sam became more worried. He was anticipating quick responses to the questions of his mind, but none came. After about an hour of intermission of silence, save for the rustling of the leaves they marched through the playground.

Dazed by what the teacher did, he didn't hesitate so long before he did what the teacher did, waiting for what the teacher would do next. The teacher crouched by an old mobile-classroom outdoors. Sam crouched too.

"Do you see this?" he pointed at a lined-up colony of ants, forming rows of ants in their numbers on two sides, while some other multitude walked gallantly in the middle moving crumbs of bread.

Surprised by what he saw, he asked, "Why did some form a

wall and are not moving, while those in the middle keep moving?"

"They are protectors of the workers who are in the middle," the teacher said with a shy smile.

"Can't they work? Does that mean they're indolent?" Sam seemed bothered by the teacher's explanation, which wasn't so detailed.

Teacher Steve unleashed raucous laughter from his mouth, "Son, that's what's called responsibility. They're so organised that each one of them in its colony understands its duty and won't leave there, even when faced with challenges."

It really touched Sam's heart that he scattered the line to confirm what the teacher just said. After about half an hour later, he couldn't curtail his delight as he jumped up in amazement to have seen that the ants never bothered about those that lost their lives, as they continued pushing the crumbs forward. He looked up at the teacher and asked, "So, what does this tell us as human, teacher?"

"We need to learn how to save during the day, so that at night, we can sit back and relax to enjoy," teacher Steve said.

"But we usually sleep at night. Or is there any other night you're talking about?" Sam asked innocently.

"The 'night' here means when we're old. Haven't you seen how miserable some people live their lives in their old age?"

"Yes, I have."

"That shows you that while they were still in their teens, they never felt they should save all the money received as incentives from families or parents. Inside the tiny brain of the ants, it thinks it should save for winter by storing up something for the future. And if I may ask you, Sam, how much have you saved so far in this first quarter of the year?" The teacher inquired looking to expunge the truth from Sam.

"I've got few quid before now that I intend saving but spent it for my guitar lesson."

"Another lesson, spend after you save and not the other way around."

Tapping Sam on his shoulder, Steve beckoned on him to follow him, and while they walked, told him to learn from that.

Sam stepped behind the teacher, and as they walked back to the school in silence, he thought w*hat a wonder the ant is!*

The teenager has a lot to learn about finance and needs to learn from the ant. So, we can succeed financially, there is a lot to learn for us all, about the tiny winy creatures:

MONEY ON ERRAND

Children can be taught at a young age that money is not real, but their way to get the things they want in life, like a messenger you send on an errand to get things done. If you have a busy home with ten or more little children and lots of work to be done, it might take you a long time to get things done; but if you employ one or two helpers to assist, this will be really helpful to get things done on time. So, the more helpers, the faster things get done. Money can be like that, just a tool to use to get things done.

Money can help you to get the things you want to achieve. But you don't say because the helpers are helping you with your house chores then you fall in love with your staff and marry your employee. That is like falling in love with money or loving money. We use cash but reserve our love for God and the people around us, not money. When we are faithful with money, then we get TRUE RICHES.

FAITHFULNESS WITH MONEY

True love often isn't just that, what often comes with it is the desire to have children. In order to responsibly do this, you need the right attitude to money beforehand, as not only will your finances be affected, but you need to pass on good spending habits and positive attitudes towards money to your children.

True riches include knowledge of the truth. If kids are not faithful with money, they will not know how to be faithful with all other important riches: loving people, discovering one's mission in life, and living to pursue the purpose why one was created.

True riches are channelled to us when we care for people, are kind to people, putting the priority of love forward, and knowing how to be faithful in things. Kids must be faithful first in worldly riches: money. They must have the right attitude towards money first. If they are not faithful with money, they cannot be faithful in other matters.

Every employer is looking for hardworking people, skillful people, who must have been tested and proven in one way or another, including money. Kids must be prepared to be faithful in all matters regarding money.

THE HISTORY OF MONEY

The first thing you need to do in order to teach your kid about money is to explain the history of money. Tell them about how people used to trade with their neighbours: "I will give you apples and you will give me carrots" kind of transactions. Then they realised that some things take longer to grow, so they decided that some things are worth more. This evolved when they came to the market to trade for the things they wanted.

The idea of money came about when people weighed pieces of gold or silver and and traded them by weight (think of the British currency, the "Pound", or the Israeli currency, "Shekel", which means "something that is weighed"). Explain to your young kid that money was a great thing that happened to us because we can buy whatever we want and not just what our neighbours grow.

THINGS TO NOTE

1. POCKET MONEY

Pocket money can often be the answer to many behavioural issues parents experience with their children [13]. Explain Pocket money – given weekly, say, in return for jobs around the house. Decide if you want to give your kids pocket money every week or as a reward for doing chores. Stick to at least once a week, because young kids' perception of time is not fully developed, and seven days seems to them like a very long time.

Some parents believe that giving pocket money should not be a reward. Others think that it is a good way to teach kids that money does not just fall from the sky and that we need to work for it. If you have difficulties finding chores for young kids, remember that small things like making the bed, helping clear the table after dinner and helping with the laundry can be fun chores that will teach children responsibility and sharing. Whatever you choose, stick to your schedule and always, hold a ceremony of giving your kids their resource.

2. EMOTIONAL CHORES

If you do choose to give money based on chores, remember you do not have to reward your kids for things they do for you. You can always reward them for things they do for themselves. "Emotional stretches" are a good reason to reward young kids (even older kids, teens and adults).

Give them coins each time they manage to do something that was hard for them. Being nice to a sibling, doing their homework without being told, taking a shower by themselves, waiting patiently when mum or dad are on the phone. Every time they do something that is hard for them, reward them to promote their good behaviour and personal growth.

3. POCKET MONEY RULES

When you choose to give pocket money as a reward, remember that the rules must be understood by everyone involved. Kids must understand how much you give and for what. If your child can read, make a list of the chores (and emotional stretches) with their matching reward amount. If your child is younger, draw pictures or cut them from a magazine and draw circles to represent the coins they will get for each task. Having an understanding will prevent bargaining, and allow both parents to handle the situation in the same way.

4. MONEY MANAGEMENT

Kids must know what falls into the category of what they need to purchase and what comes out of mum and dad's budget. Think about this before you start teaching your kid about money. You must be clear with yourself whether you pay for food, for snacks at school, for sweets, for treats or for anything else the kids ask for. Whatever you decide is good, as long as you have a good explanation for yourself and you stick to it.

5. PIGGY BANK

Get your child a box to put their money in. Any piggy bank that does not allow the kids to take the money out is a cruel thing for your kid. It does the exact opposite of what money management is all about. Money is not there to keep. It is there to use wisely.

A piggy bank is a good way to teach your child mathematics and the importance of saving. With the coins in a piggy bank, you can teach your child counting, subtraction or addition. If you are using a piggy bank to teach younger children math, make sure to count the coin loudly as they drop in the till. Older children can learn addition by adding up the money they have collected. They can also learn subtraction by removing a certain amount from the money to buy something.

Today, online banking applications are available in which you can set up a digital 'savings pot' for your children. If you approach this with the right attitude with your children, you can make this into a fun activity.

Allow them to monitor their 'savings pot' with your supervision. Allow them to check it each week and motivate them to keep adding to it.

By making this into a fun activity, you are encouraging your children to have a 'bigger picture' mindset.

6. LESS IS SOMETIMES MORE

Young kids find it hard to understand that a £1/ $1 coin is worth more than 20 coins of 5 pence/5 cents each. It takes a while for them to understand that the value of the money is not measured by the number of coins. Therefore, always use the smallest coins to give them money, to give them the feeling they have plenty of money.

Around the age of 6, when they learn the arithmetic of money at school, they will learn the value of each coin. When they do understand this, start exchanging single pence/cents for 10 pence/10 cents, 10 pence/cents for 25 or 50 pence/cents, and 50 pence/cents for pounds/dollars, etc.

7. WALLET

Get your kid a wallet to take with them whenever you go out. When a young kid takes a wallet with them for shopping, this is the greatest lesson about money management. When you go shopping and your kid asks for you to buy them things, refer them to their wallet and explain what they can buy with the money that they have.

Always show them the options, "This costs this many coins, another thing you want costs that many coins," and teach them to choose. When they see the money going out of their own wallet, they are not so enthusiastic about buying things, and if they are still enthusiastic, the feeling disappears after the first time when they realise they have no money left in their wallet.

8. LOANS

If you go with your kid somewhere and they did not bring their wallet, use the opportunity to teach them about lending and let them borrow some money until you get home. Only lend them amounts they can return and make sure they give you the money back the minute you get home.

If they have their wallet with them but not enough money, and they ask for an allowance, make sure they understand what this means. Again, time is not something they understandand if you tell them, "That means that next month I will not give you your pocket money." They might not understand.

Just like in real life, teach them that things that require loans also require more time to think about. In these cases, not giving them the loan, or giving part of the loan is better for your kids than being nice and giving it to them whenever they want.

9. SAVINGS

The first time your young children ask you for a loan, be happy, because now you can teach them about savings. See, it's only when they begin to truly interact with money and develop a desire for it, that you should approach the subject. Only when kids want something beyond their financial means can you explain why saving money is a good idea. Teach them to always put at least 10% of their money aside. 10%, though it doesn't sound like much, is a consistent rate of saving that is healthier long-term than saving huge amounts sporadically. It's also better than dedicating an exact financial number, like £100 per month, as it means the number you save will increase in line with inflation.

At a young age, they will not understand what 10% is, but tell them that it is a tiny piggy bank in the piggy bank of money you keep there for emergency. Alternatively, you can use the digital 'savings pot' we talked about earlier too (this will have a similar effect, and may just scratch their digital itch for using technology). The 10% you save will be the money you keep for something big or special that you want later. Tell them to put one out of every ten coins in the tiny piggy bank. Saving is a good lesson in waiting, something that is hard for young kids because their perception of time is not fully formed.

Right behind the subject of birds and bees is talking to kids about money; and money is one of the most difficult conversations for parents. Deciding what to tell them about earning, savings and growing cash can be a difficult task, mainly since many of us were never given money management skills at home and perhaps still do not know a whole lot about the subject in thefirst place.

This book provides you with a framework to discuss money with your kids, and will help you establish a foundation to share your values about finance with them. The current economic and credit crisis is, at the very least, anecdotal evidence that our views on money need some improvement, especially if we hope our children will not repeat our mistakes and will, therefore, become good earners, savers and stewards of their own resources.

A recent survey among secondary/high school and university students revealed kids pick up their views and values about money and finances at home, largely through observation and by hearing their parents talk about money. In other words, whether we intentionally teach them or not, our kids will learn the good and the bad we have to offer regarding financial matters.

Clearly, it would be a great step for us to make this process more deliberate and ensure the way we see money, and what we teach our children about it help them in the long run.

THE NEW METAPHOR

Money is energy. This is a metaphor we need to understand and communicate to our kids. We live in great countries where many people have started with nothing and have built up amazing fortunes. Many others have lost it all overnight due to corporate failures, fraud or poor judgment.

For some others, however, money is what keeps a roof over the heads, gives comfort, or even keeps up at night if they do not have what they need. For these reasons, money is typically a very emotional subject. For some, money is insecurity, pain and shame. For others, money is pride, greed, fun and excitement.

None of these emotions are ultimately healthy when they are attached to the way we see money. And whether we like it or not, we tend to pass on these emotionally charged views on money as part of our values to our children during their upbringing.

Would you like to see your children grow in gup, afraid of money, or having an unhealthy attachment to what money represents in terms of material things or immediate gratification? My guess is you probably would not. This is why we need a different metaphor when we discuss money. It is nothing to be feared or pursued obsessively.

Money is just energy. Energy is neutral and is all around us in the physical world. The cash and the credit/debit cards we keep in our pockets are just expressions of money. Imagine that you need four pints of milk. Getting it is really simple: you reach into your pocket and use a few pounds/dollars to buy your milk at the store. But what would happen if you could not get anyone to sell you milk in exchange for your money? You would have to put in a lot of hard work to obtain it, perhaps driving to a distant dairy farm or raising a cow yourself! That would certainly take a lot of valuable time and energy from you.

In modern times, we do not have to take such drastic measures to procure a measly four pints of milk. We have figured out that it is far more efficient for each of us to specialise in our own functions (jobs) and trade units of energy (cash) in exchange for our labour and for what we need (food and shelter). This is a simple formula that works to optimize the flow and use of energy of our society. Meaning, the farmer who has the milk sells it to the supermarket, then the supermarket sells the milk to us - we all have different jobs/functions in the process. In other words, money is energy; and we get to have an amount that is proportional to how much of energy we give out to the world.

THE PROPERTIES OF ENERGY AND MONEY

Any science book will tell you that energy has four key properties: it can be transferred, it can take multiple forms, it can be only converted from one form to another, and because of that, it can never be created or destroyed.

If you think about it, money has much in common with energy, as it can be transferred and it can be converted into many forms. Now, can money be created or destroyed? Technically, yes. You could take all your cash and burn it in the living room fireplace, but this is not the right way to think about it. A more logical approach to the indestructibility of money is as follows:

Imagine you are a frontiers man or woman and you arrive to the vast plains of Montana in the 1800s. Through much labour and hard work, you convert a big expanse of land into a productive farm and as a result, you emerge as a wealthy land owner and farmer. You did not destroy the land, you transformed it. Before you arrived, the energy of that land was serving nature and the animals of the region. Now it belongs to you and you can turn its bounty into cash and become a rich person. You took the energy of your work and the gift of nature and transformed them into a cash machine.

We can come up with many other examples, including inventions and new ways of doing business (such as the Internet), but I think you get the point. Energy and money are very close relatives!

What you do with the two and how you make them apply to your life is what really matters. The possibilities are truly endless.

THE EDUCATIONAL VALUE

There is educational value of seeing money as energy. One of the most important milestones in the mental development of children is when they finally make an unequivocal connection between cause and effect in the key areas of their life. Some popular examples include: if they touch fire they get burned; if they do not finish their homework, they get a terrible grade; if they are helpful around the house, they score a nice allowance.

Money is a subject that requires cause and effect thinking in order to be understood and mastered. What is most important for kids and young people to grasp is that behaviour has a direct impact on a person's ability to accumulate wealth. There is nothing mysterious about it; it is cause and effect in action. In other words, there are certain skills and actions that attract more money to us (saving, budgeting, investing, etc.), and there are others that push money away from us (overspending, abusing credit cards, etc.). It is that simple.

In today's society, where social media and other such digital marketing strategies are constantly in your face when you use internet-enabled digital devices - it can be difficult to avoid those aspects of technology that distract you from positive spending and saving.

To illustrate this point, here are some common statements children hear about money. The way these statements are presented is based on emotion and not on logical or cause-and-effect thinking. These emotionally charged statements diminish your children's ability to think about money logically and are likely to seed in them negative beliefs about wealth, which could seriously affect them in the future. See if you can spot the logical flaws before reading the explanation:

1. "That family has money, we don't."

This is something we previously mentioned earlier in the book, and is likely going to be something you will hear at least a few times throughout your child's years, particularly as a teenager. While it is probably true that a particular family is presently wealthier than your own, a statement like this presents a relative condition (they have more than us right now) as absolute and unchangeable. To the impressionable mind of a child, it may sound as a permanent reality and imply he comes from a family cursed with misfortune.

It is far better and more productive to avoid comparisons with other people and establish that your current situation can be changed. Focus on discussing possible actions that can improve the conditions of the family, such as avoiding unnecessary expenses, reading books about investing, brainstorming business ideas, etc.

2. "If you want to have money, you have to work hard."

Money, how you choose to earn it and and how much you earn is not necessarily determined by skill, talent or even drive. Therefore, this statement is only partially true, and is therefore extremely deceptive. Hard work can produce financial rewards and many wealthy people worked very hard to build and preserve their fortune. However, hard work is another absolute view that negates other possibilities. For example, there are many people who worked hard to find the right opportunity, but did not have to struggle so much once they positioned themselves properly.

This is how many fortunes in the Internet were created. Others were lost because some people put their heads down and worked hard without looking out for changes in the horizon. Hard work alone does not create wealth. It is only through a combination of smart work and hard work that we can succeed. Each one of them alone is not enough; you need both.

Most kids don't work hard because they do not see dignity in labour. Ben was a 17-year-old boy who looked for summer holiday job. When he could not find any, his father advised him to go and help out in his uncle's office. But he refused, because the organization was not going to pay him. He told his friend about that in a jesting manner, but his friend Alex went for the job while he sat at home eating.

Alex did the work from 9am to 5pm everyday, without pay;

yet he liked the dignity of working; a wage or salary was not his motivation. His motivation was that the experience will add growth to him; he would gain new knowledge, a working knowledge of the trade which he did.

Many years after his graduation when a lot of people were being laid off work, Alex was such a treasure to his employer because of his attitude to work that he could not be laid off; rather, he had an increase in his contract.

3. "You need money to make money."

This is a statement that is probably responsible for stalling the dreams of many people around the world. It is technically true, but is deceptive as well. The technicality is that you need investment funds to launch a new business, but the funds do not necessarily have to come from you; they can come from investors.

If the creator of a new great business idea does not have the money, there are ways to obtain it. There are countless examples of people with creative ability who started a business with an idea, and managed to convince others to invest in them, give them free advertising, etc. Today, there is a multi-billion dollar industry of venture capitalists who pour billions every year, regardless of what the economy is doing, into new business ventures that have potential. Many fail, but they only need a few to succeed to make it worth their while.

If you teach your kids that a good idea is worth a fortune (instead of telling them the statement above), you will free them to think, meditate, conceive and create. Actually, I would like to offer you a better statement: "You need salesmanship to make money." This is a lot more accurate in the world of business.

Many good ideas go nowhere because the creator does not know how to convince others on the merits of his or her creation. The good news is salesmanship is a learnable skill. Make your kids aware of the importance of a good, persuasive and polished presentation and you may be opening for them the golden doors of success.

The truth of the matter is that in the modern digital age of today, you can get your ideas recognised much easier and cheaper - not only via marketing them on social media but in terms of actually financing your idea.

Crowdfunding campaigns have proved very popular and largely successful over the last ten years and can give you that crucial first step onto the business ladder. Working by encouraging visitors of your page to pledge their hard-earned money to your cause (your business idea). How do you do this? By giving people different rewards, depending on how much money they choose to pledge.

So, there you have it, you don't need money to make money - you can rely on the community of the internet, accessible to people across the world, to fund your project and help with your journey to success.

4. "Rich people are rarely happy."

For a start, poor people are rarely happy as well. In fact, human beings are seldom happy. Many articles online will tell you only rich people are unhappy, or at least give you the many reasons why they usually aren't happy [14]. Happiness is an emotional skill that is not connected to money in anyway. It has to do with our ability to manage our emotions and be well adjusted to our environment. There are many books written on the subject of happiness and how to obtain it. But, trust me, money is a very small factor.

Unless we are talking about dying of an untreated disease or starvation, money is not going to put a durable smile on your face. What it will do is give you more choices, offer you interesting experiences, get you peace of mind regarding your bills and, hopefully, give you a chance to contribute to charitable causes.

Do not look for happiness in money; instead, accept that you like money and teach your children that it is okay to want to have money and the opportunities it provides. Do not deny the practical benefits of having money just because it can not give you happiness. Money and happiness are simply not connected. If you want more happiness and joy, get to know yourself from your creator's perspective, work hard on your personal growth of knowing this, and teach your kids to do the same.

Love God, and that went with love for people, was the main desire for Joyce, a 16-year-old girl; and this was the reason why she looked for a job in T-Mobile and she sent all her money to a Charity. She did so to free herself from the love of money.

She had been equipped with the richness of knowledge about money such that money does not make her happy or sad; money is not in control of her. She had been so trained that money does not change her mood; it does not make her happy or sad. Money does not determine her goals or happiness, it does not determine her time either, as she works part time and it does not determine how much she spends with her family or at work.

5. "I have no idea how to make or grow my money."

I could not agree with this more! You do not know before you know. What I mean is that this is something you need to learn. It is not in our genes and it is not intuitive. Becoming a savvy saver, investor, etc is not automatic. These are skills that take time to master. But do not get discouraged by that. Instead, get used to saying that you do not know it yet, but you will eventually if you learn.

Many worthwhile skills take a lifetime to master. Think about parenthood, for example. We do not come into this world with a clear idea of what it is like to be parents, but we learn. Trial and error or getting some coaching on the subject can help. We read books about parenting or even books such as this one.

But wait, maybe you could do the same with financial skills. Just realise it is a learnable skill and that a lot of progress can be made through reading or by finding a practical person (mentor). The sooner you start, the better. Introduce your child to someone who does well with money, or give them a book about financial literacy and you will probably change their lives forever.

Put your plan to teach your kids about money in action. Remember this, and whether you consciously teach your kids about money or not, they are picking up your beliefs and values on this subject already; so why not take charge of the process? Take the following simple steps and see how they work for you:

- Read this part or chapter a couple of times until you get the principles in it.
- Think about the beliefs you picked up from your own parents growing up.
- Decide which of these beliefs are helpful to build a financially free future.
- Choose the beliefs you like and let go of those that are not helpful.
- Have a conversation with your kids about money and share your values with them.
- Offer them a good book and help them find a good mentor. If you can be the mentor, even better.

FINANCIAL TIPS FOR KIDS

Here is the title of this book, and offers us a good reason to look more closely into it. So far, the point has been made that kids need financial intelligence to give them a proper headstart about money as a tool everyone needs to have a good wellbeing in this life.

An undeniable truth today is that although teenagers everywhere are faced with so many new learning experiences, yet one of the most important aspects of their adult life (personal finance) is not adequately covered for most kids prior to their secondary/high school graduation.

In today's hi-tech, hi-test, supercharged video game era, it's difficult to get kids' attention long enough to get them to clean their rooms, not to mention learn something about finances.

CREATIVE WAYS TO TALK ABOUT MONEY

After many bouts of trial and error, below are Financial Tips to teach kids, and a few creative ways to get their attention while doing so.

1. BANKING

Open a savings account for your child at birth and start developing your lesson plan for teaching money matters. During their teenage years open a bank account, but do not give them full reign on this account. Start by teaching the basics of deposits and withdrawals, using cheques and deposit slips. Teach them how to reconcile the account, noting that the balance on the online system may not be their actual balance.

Add a debit card when appropriate, but be very careful with this part of the lesson. It can be very costly if kids get carried away with the flow of cash from a cash machine/ online transactions that are not tracked properly.

2. TALK ABOUT MONEY MATTERS

Years ago, it was considered taboo to discuss your personal finances with your kids. In today's financial times, it is imperative that you discuss the basics and more. Making your kids comfortable with the topic starts with you getting comfortable discussing money matters first.

Start with basic conversations about savings, budgeting and banking. Use your real life experiences such as bank fees that you notice on your bank statement. Share your strategy on how you plan to reduce or eliminate those fees going forward. You'll be surprised how much children engage when you start including them in what used to be considered a "grown ups only" discussion.

3. BASIC BUDGETING

Start teaching kids basic budgeting skills early; and as they grow, progressively increase the lessons to the point of developing their own budget. Basic money management requires that you track your spending and identify where your funds are going. This is one of the biggest tips you will teach your children. This is a simple process that once it becomes a habit it will prove to be very beneficial to them over time.

4. NEEDS VS. WANTS

Making a difference between needs and wants to a child can be challenging because teenagers think everything they want is a need. Help them identify the basics of food, shelter and clothing (not the latest fashion). Although they may be able to get an item that they want but don't necessarily need, make sure they understand that it should be included in their budget in order for them to make the purchase.

Modern digital marketing strategies often blur the lines between what 'want' and 'need' really mean, bombarding you with sponsored posts on Instagram and 'suggested for you' marketing on Facebook - there truly is no escape. You have quite the challenge on your hands in tackling the blurred lines between social media and other such digital marketing and the importance of saving your money for what you need/savings towards something bigger and more important.

5. CREDIT CARD

Teach your kids that credit should NOT be used; but where it has to be used, it has to be with care. Help them understand how buying something they want (but don't necessarily need) on credit now could result in acquiring too much debt, leading to problems later. Use the credit card statement as a teaching tool to share the concept of simple versus compound interest.

Show your teens that only about 15% of each minimum payment goes toward the principal balance and the remaining 85% goes towards interest. They need to understand that a £3,000/$3,000 balance could take close to 40 years to pay off if they pay the minimum payment each month.

6. UNDERSTANDING CREDIT SCORES

Most people, not to mention teenagers, are clueless about credit scores and how to establish and maintain good credit. Credit scores reflect how well you manage your credit. The scores are similar to the grades that students receive in school. Teach your children the types of credit relationships to establish and maintain, primarily with banks. Encourage them to always strive for A credit by paying their bills on time and not obtaining too much credit.

7. INVEST NOW

Investing is a tool that can be taught early. Teach your teens that people have ownership in various companies such as British Petroleum, Amazon, Microsoft, Apple, Walmart, Xerox and the local cable stations. They can also have ownership in these companies by purchasing stock. As an assignment, have them research different companies or industries of interest.

Have them investigate various investment options like mutual funds, stocks and bonds that might allow them to gain ownership into some of their favorite industries or companies. Now make monthly investments that should prove to be rewarding by the time they reach their thirties.

8. SECURING VALUABLES

Teach your teens that their identity is just as valuable as the items or cash that they try to safeguard and protect. By now, they may be in a position to complete applications or forms that require their social security number.

Explain the importance of not sharing their social security number, account numbers or personal identification numbers with others. Sometimes kids think that sharing this information with their best friend is okay. Explain that this is not negotiable. Identity theft is prevalent in today's society and they don't want to become a victim.

9. KEEP IT INTERESTING

To help keep your teaching moments interesting, consider playing games like Monopoly which teaches the advantages of owning property; this shows them how their assets will start to work for them. While you're at it, teach your teens how to make changes without depending on a cash register or calculator.

10. GET ALLOWANCE, PAY YOUR OWN WAY

Have you ever noticed how fast kids can spend your money? They really do believe that your finances or endless, or that you're somehow rich just because you have a job and they don't.

Give your kids the responsibility of paying their own way and watch the spending decline. Allow them to earn an allowance that require them to be responsible for a bill such as their mobile/cell phone or weekly dinner/lunch money. Make sure you enforce the budgeting process to ensure they understand their role. You will be amazed how those spending habits change when the money comes from their wallet.

In today's society, your child may have a Spotify subscription, so you could suggest that they pay for this with the money they earn.

As adults we all want the best for our children. Ensuring that they are prepared for life is one of our most prominent roles as parents. Planning to spend as much quality time as possible on finance will interest teens. These ten exercises will give more opportunities to spend quality time teaching finance as one of life's lessons.

DAMIEN

Damien's parents took this advice and ran with it, giving Damien more financial responsibility in order to improve his work ethic and teach him the value of money.

Damien had a real passion for gaming and would spend much of his leisure time on his Xbox. Of course, as you likely know, playing against people in multiplayer games such as Call of Duty, Fortnite and Halo, unfortunately costs a significant subscription price. Priced at around £6 per month or £40 per year, this is a significant cost for any parent, but Damien's parents ensured the cost was covered - teaching Damien valuable life lessons in the process.

For a year's subscription, Damien had agreed to do one important/large-scale job around the house per week. If he didn't do the job, the Xbox would be confiscated for the following week.

Knowing the rules, Damien knew not to step out of line and was driven to keep his Xbox Live subscription, so would always keep up to his weekly tasks.

HOW TO BE SUCCESSFUL CHILDREN

This Chapter title puts the onus and responsibility of becoming financially independent on the child to make himself or herself successful. That's as it gets to be at the end of the day. But parents share that responsibility in the immediate present time. We are to set our children on the path of that successful life.

What you say and do about money has a profound influence on your child. There are money moments every day that you can use to teach your children essential skills and lessons about life. But what to say or do isn't always obvious.

Is it a good idea to pay for chores or grades? How do you help your child develop a work ethic? How do you structure an allowance to help your child learn to make choices? Why is involving your children in charity so important?

EIGHT BEHAVIOURS OF SUCCESSFUL PEOPLE

There are eight crucial behaviors that will help parents raise financially responsible children:

1. ENCOURAGE A WORK ETHIC

Work ethic is a learned behaviour, and parents are the best models to teach kids to acquire it. If you want your children to work hard and derive meaning and satisfaction from what they do, make sure you are modeling the right messages. Insisting your kids do their homework and help around the house does not guarantee they will grow up with a sense of accountability and a desire to achieve. But get them to work. Work is good!

2. GET YOUR OWN MONEY STORIES STRAIGHT

Because you send your children messages about money all the time, it is imperative that both you and your spouse are on the same page when it comes to your money stories.

A money story is an open, honest and personal story of your relationship with financial issues, especially as you grew up, because most people's relationship with money developed during childhood. You need to identify why you feel the way you do about money so you can send coherent and consistent messages to your kids.

When both parents focus on their money stories, children receive positive messages. Getting your money stories straight does not just mean that you agree on basic issues such as allowances and university savings. It also means that both of you have agreed to identify certain basic money values you want to teach your children, such as giving is good, working hard has its reward, and you don't always get everything you want.

3. FACILITATE FINANCIAL REFLECTION

As with most decisions kids make, when it comes to money decisions, they are frequently impulsive. As a financially intelligent parent, you want to teach your children how to think in terms of choices, alternatives and consequences. This is called reflective thinking.

Learning how to reflect both before and after making a decision is a great life skill, and one that is the hallmark of people who make good choices in everything from careers to relationships to investments. Financially intelligent parents teach their children to evaluate financial consequences based on available choices rather than making impulsive decisions. As a result, children recognise that there are many options available and they acquire the skill to make good choices.

4. BECOME A CHARITABLE FAMILY

By teaching your children that they can do more with money than spend it on themselves, you encourage them to become more compassionate and caring. By participating as a family in volunteer and community activities, you help your children develop empathy and a sense of responsibility to others.

Your children will realise that they have the power to make life better for others. Because children learn through modeling behaviour, you have to do more than write a cheque to charity. You need to show your children what it means to help others. Modeling charitable behaviors, including volunteerism, can jumpstart your child's empathy and desire to help others.

Today, finding the right charitable organisation to support is easier than ever. The internet is a fantastic resource in learning about all the possible organisations out there that you could choose to pledge money to. Not only do most organisations have websites, but they also have public-access documents, readily-available for you to read. Ten to twenty years ago, this wouldn't have been information that you were privy to, but now it's open season on information. You have a vast library of knowledge available at your fingertips, thanks to your digital devices.

5. TEACH FINANCIAL LITERACY

Although it is crucial to teach children how to balance a chequebook and create a budget, to become truly financially literate your children must learn within a context of values and money behaviors. Your children need a combination of concrete examples, their own experiences and financial reflection. If they do not learn to behave responsibly with money as kids, they will have to learn as adults when the cost is much higher.

One of the best tools to teach your children financial literacy is an allowance. Approaching allowances in a consistently constructive way allows you to instil decision-making wisdom in your children, rather than controlling them. An allowance also helps your children gain a well-balanced perspective about money, encouraging saving, investing and giving, in addition to spending.

6. AWARENESS OF THE VALUES YOU MODEL

Your children are tuned in to your purchasing decisions. The ways you spend your money sends messages to your children about your values and life priorities. Children also notice how you spend your time; and your actions can unintentionally send messages you did not intend your children to receive.

When you miss opportunities to spend time with your children in order to put in extra hours at work, or manage your money, you are sending a message that money is more important than family. Financially intelligent parents are highly conscious of their spending habits, as well as how they balance their work and family time, and the values they communicate.

7. MODERATE EXTREME MONEY TENDENCIES

Extreme money tendencies can evolve into money disorders which cause chaos within your family, and send the wrong messages to your children.

There are several types of money disorders, ranging from excessive shopping to racking up credit card debt, to excessive frugality. Regardless of the disorder, extreme money tendencies cause your children to experience confusion and insecurity in their lives. Financially intelligent parents learn to recognise and moderate extreme money behaviours.

You also need to take into account the possibility that extreme money tendencies may just be a symptom of severe depression. Take a look at your child (or anybody in your life with money troubles) and assess their situation. Ask yourself if they are spending unhealthy durations of time on digital devices. Ask yourself if they go out and see their friends often enough. If you suspect there is an issue, always encourage them to speak to a medical professional.

8. TALKING ABOUT THE TOUGH TOPICS

Parents avoid talking about financial topics that make them uncomfortable or that seem too complicated. Although you model good money behaviours in certain ways, unless you compliment these behaviours with good money conversations, you are not going to be as effective as you should be.

Financially intelligent parents recognise teachable times each day that give you and your children the opportunity to talk about financial issues. You should welcome these opportunities, as difficult as they are, to discuss and reflect on financial decisions.

TONY

Tony, from Goole, UK, is a parent who experienced first-hand just how uncomfortable it can be to approach the difficult subjects with children.

He noticed that as his son got a part-time job (when he turned 17), his spending became more frivolous than ever before. This was likely due to the fact that he had never really been given any kind of financial freedom or responsibility, but nevertheless, the way he was spending money was unhealthy.

Tony approached the subject with his son, but with a heavy heart. He told him a story of how he had a really good job when he was younger.

"I worked for a really high-profile tech company when I was in my twenties. I thought I was set for life, they had very big plans and we all thought they were going to take over the world." Tony explained.

"I never really saved anything because I always thought I'd continue to rise through the ranks there, I thought I was safe. Then, the next thing I knew, I was turning up to work one morning and the offices were boarded up. The owners had sold up to an even bigger firm, and we were all made redundant, effective immediately".

Tony really hammered home the point that just because you have a job and you're earning money, it doesn't mean you always will. You should save while things are good.

WHAT YOUR KIDS SHOULD KNOW

Most people learn about finance the hard way through mistakes made from practical experience. People usually aren't taught about personal finance in school. Moreover, parents don't teach their children the basics either because they don't understand it themselves, or they don't take the time to do it. So, most of us learn about money as we go through life. We make purchases, go into debt, and end up with a meagre resignation account.

BASIC FINANCIAL PRINCIPLES

What if they had made better financial decisions earlier in their life? Perhaps if they were told about some basic financial principles, they would be in a better position? Here are some basic financial principles that your kids should know to avoid making simple mistakes:

1. DON'T SPEND BEYOND YOUR MEANS.

This is such a basic principle that it would not seem to be worth mentioning; however, it is the key principle to financial success. Most financial advisors will tell you to pay yourself first by saving 6-10% of your income. You can only do that if you spend less than you make. So the first and perhaps most important rule of financial success is not to spend beyond your means.

2. SAVE FOR A RAINY DAY.

As we talked about in Tony's case, this is a particularly important point and one that children need to be aware of - despite it potentially scaring them. As soon as you start working, open a savings account as an emergency fund, a rainy day fund. A rule of thumb is to have a reserve equivalent to six month's salary in case you are out of work and (for investment).

If you have an emergency, like a major car repair or medical bill, you would need to replenish the fund if you pay your bills using your emergency savings account.

3. TEACH YOUR CHILDREN TO BE GENEROUS AND SERVE OTHERS.

How can your children serve others? Children can serve others by volunteering, helping the family, helping their friends and making a difference in society. Children who serve others feel as if they have a meaningful life, and this makes them happy. Another thing that makes children happy is generosity. Children are happy when they can help others. So, motivate your children to serve others and be generous.

I told the story of Kelly in my book *101 Tips for Child Development.* Kelly and his father went shopping in the supermarket. At the mall, Kelly met a young boy about his age crying. Kelly's dad asked of his parent. The small boy pointed to a short middle-aged man talking to the cashier. Then, Kelly's dad asked why he was crying. He said his father promised to buy him a wristwatch if he had good grades in his exam and he did. When they got to the supermarket, he knew his father does not have the money to buy him a wristwatch.

Kelly, without thinking twice, removed the wristwatch his mum got him for his eleventh birthday which he celebrated the past month and stretched it to the boy. The boy looked at Kelly, then at the wristwatch, but did not take it.

"Don't you like it?" Kelly asked.

"Yes, I do, but it's yours."

"Don't worry, you can have it."

"Really? Are you serious?"

"Yes, please. I have another one at home."

The boy then took the wristwatch happily, and ran to his father. Both father and son came to Kelly and his father. The boy's father, almost in tears, thanked Kelly and his father. The boy and his father left the supermarket happily.

"Why did you do that?" Kelly's dad asked him as soon as the boy and his dad left.

"Nothing, I just felt that I needed to help the boy, plus my teacher taught me from John 13:29 that Jesus used money for only two things, one was to buy what he needed and two was to help the needy. He was crying and I couldn't bear that," Kelly said unflinchingly.

I can imagine the excitement on Kelly's dad's face; but at the same time, I have the instinct that Kelly learnt that from his parents.

Over time, by setting positive, giving examples for children, parents can help mould their young adult into well-rounded individuals. Just like in this scenario, I bet that you will be surprised just how much your child has been learning just from watching you.

12

HOW TO RAISE KIDS SUCCEESFULLY

If you have read *101 Tips for Child Development,* then you probably know how passionate I am about raising kids the right way. I believe that how a person is in adulthood is largely influenced by how he or she was raised as a kid.

When kids do not get positive feedback and a nurturing environment from at least one parent, the tendency is to seek acceptance and attention somewhere else – oftentimes it's through peers. Then when they become out of control, teens will think it's normal process that they go through, and going through teens is the most challenging part because it is at this stage that they are in between childhood and adulthood and on the path of finding their identity.

PROCEDURES FOR SUCCESSFUL PARENTING

Successful parenting can be achieved by all; and no matter what the situation is, it can be corrected. Here are some sound words that can help you achieve this:

1. GIVE UNCONDITIONAL LOVE AND POSITIVE ATTENTION

Love your children just for being your kids, not because they excelled in school or sports, not just because they show talent, but just for being your kids. Give them ample attention. Communicate a lot. Give hugs or reassuring touches. Take time to listen to them. Attend school functions. Enjoy activities with them. Do things together, whether it's a fun activity or house chores.

Kids love and seek their parents' attention – whether they get it in a positive or negative behaviour depends on what the parents reinforce. If they don't get the positive attention and acceptance from parents, they will always seek it somewhere else, and peers are their most likely recourse. Create a stronger bond with your kids and they will always gravitate towards that bond.

2. CREATE A POSITIVE ENVIRONMENT WITHIN EVERY KID

As kids grow, they need affirmation of what they are doing; it reinforces a habit or behavior. So always keep in mind to praise good work and achievement, no matter how little those successes will be – to them it can mean so much already, and this builds confidence in them. Support their interest and encourage them in what aptitude or talent you can see in your child.

Conversely, when they do something wrong or unpleasant, do not just reprimand without letting them know why, and if you have to reprimand, do it as calm as possible and in private – humiliation, especially in front of others creates low self-worth and resentment, and a possible start of a hostile behaviour. Also, NEVER compare one kid with another. Always remember that every kid is unique and has his or her own abilities or traits.

3. TEACH THEM RESPONSIBILITY

Love, but do not pamper. Even as little kids they have to learn responsibility, like putting away their toys, making their bed, setting aside time for studies, even sharing little bits of housework. This in particular does two things: you teach them responsibility, and it serves as a bonding activity as well.

Teaching kids responsibility also can be done by showing them that receiving something they want is sometimes a reward for a positive behaviour, and that in their little way they "worked" for what they received. It gives positive reinforcement and encouragement for a deed or action.

4. TEACH THEM TO BE KIND, HELPFUL AND TO APPRECIATE WHAT THEY HAVE

Kind, helpful and appreciative are likely none of the qualities you think about when you think of the modern child of the digital age. Unfortunately, social media and digital technologies, though definitely have their benefits, unfortunately create tensions and issues that wouldn't have even been a factor ten to twenty years ago. For the most part, it seems as though we're constantly giving in to children, whether it be buying them the latest technology, or dealing with an issue caused by something they've seen on digital technology. That's why it's more important than ever to go back to basics and teach the valuable qualities a person should have.

Teaching your kid to be kind and helpful creates a gentle spirit within. Similarly, letting them appreciate whatever they have will create a positive outlook. When my kids were growing up and we saw unfortunate or unpleasant situations, I always told them how blessed they are that they were not in the same situation; but at the same time, seeing how blessed they are, they should pass it forward by kindness. The best way to show this is when they see this in you!

5. GIVE THEM THE GIFT OF INNER STRENGTH

Give your kids the gift of inner strength, to accept mistakes, rejection and failure in a constructive way. Kids need to know that it is normal to fail (and not being scolded for it!), and making mistakes is a good exercise to teach us inner strength. Adverse things happen in life sometimes, and the important thing is that one did ONE'S best, not THE best, and to learn from these mistakes instead of sulking and pondering over these mistakes.

Another significant way we can teach our kids inner strength is by not giving in to all they want. As parents we are sometimes guilty of doing this, but instant gratification every time will not build the kids' character. Rather, we are to help them realise that they cannot have everything they want. This should be explained thoughtfully.

It's worth noting that many aspects of the digital age are orientated around bringing people down.

Negativity on the internet is a plague, so teaching your child about their inner strength, money related or not, is crucial.

6. PUT MOTIVATION IN A POSITIVE PERSPECTIVE

When you encourage your kid to do things, especially in

studies, teach your kid the value of doing his best, instead of negative programming – "study or you are grounded". This makes for a negative, short-term motivation, and will not teach your kid the value on his future.

7. TO A CERTAIN DEGREE, INVOLVE THEM WITH THE SITUATION AT HAND

How you handle this will depend on the kids' age — knowing the proper timing and manner how to say this is crucial. Are you having certain financial struggles? Serious problems? While these are adult problems, they can be communicated to the kid to a certain extent.

If done appropriately, it gives children a solid grasp of reality. The key here is to explain it in the least negative way possible without showing bitterness but rather acceptance and optimism.

8. LEARN TO SAY SORRY

As adults and parents, we are not infallible. Sometimes a sudden burst of anger from a parent, or a false accusation, will cause a child to feel dejected. Learn to apologise to them, as it teaches the child to be humble and do the same when wrong.

Good parenting involves a lot of love, patience and communication. The key is developing a close positive relationship with your kids. We only get one shot at raising our kids – once they grow up crooked, it becomes hard to correct. The greatest gift we can give our kids therefore is raising them with the proper values, attitude and character.

INTRODUCTION TO ENTREPRENEURSHIP

In this final chapter of this book, I want to touch on a matter I have skirted around in the preceding chapters: Entreprenuership.

A ONE-SIDED SYSTEM

Does talking to children about entrepreneurship at an early age make sense? Our school system is set up to lead our children into the workplace as employees, not employers. Now don't get me wrong, as a society we definitely need employees: police officers, firefighters, doctors, nurses, etc., but why not shine some light on entrepreneurship too?

Incorporating the principles and philosophy of success with emphasis on teamwork, community involvement, and entrepreneurship will no doubt go well with all types of learners of varying ages. Children deserve the opportunity to at least hear about what entrepreneurship is, why they may want to be entrepreneurial, when they could do this and, of course, how to be an entrepreneur.

We find that children are very responsive when talking about being resourceful on their own. As early as six years of age, children are starting to realise the importance behind making your own resources versus working for someone else. Unfortunately, not enough children in the world are being introduced to this kind of lifestyle.

STEPS TO ENTREPRENUERSHIP

Below are some great tips, in no particular order, to help you introduce your child to entrepreneurship.

1. STORY TIME

A great way to get your child started is by sharing with them inspiring stories of kids today who are already entrepreneurs. The internet is a great resource, making available great stories about kid entrepreneurs from around the world, what they are doing right now and how they are doing it.

When sharing inspiring kid entrepreneur stories, ask your children questions like, How did they do that? Why did they do it? Do you think you can do something like that? What makes you feel that way? If you get an answer like, "I can't do that," then ask a follow-up question: Well, if you could do that, how would you do it?" This usually gets a response like, "Oh!" And whatever follows that, don't forget to show your kids pictures, or watch videos or check out newsclips of kid entrepreneurs. It's also quite effective when kids hear the stories right from another kid's mouth.

2. DAY OUT/SCHOOL TRIP FUN

Contact local businesses or news agencies to see if you could arrange for your kids to visit with them and get a behind-the-scenes look at how the particular business operates. Approach businesses that hold a high-interest level for your kids. Let the places know that you are interested in a behind-the-scenes look at their business' operations for your child/children and their friends who are learning about entrepreneurship.

I highly recommend that you bring your children's friends too, so you all can enjoy the experience together so that your child has likeminded individuals to discuss their finding with.

3. FUNDRAISER

Have a fundraiser for a cause that is very important to your child or have them pick products they think they can sell either in the neighborhood or to local businesses. Let your kids bring in some of their friends that want to be a part of the action.

Have them brainstorm ideas and narrow the list down to a few that they all agree on. Assist them in organising the timing and the locations they conduct these "business meetings."

4. MAKE PLANNING FUN

Start planning with your kids. For the younger kids create a plan book from scratch, even some of the older kids can get into this too. Design it however they want. They can add stickers or make fancy title pages within their planner. The point here is for them to personalise it as much as they like.

You can even pick up an inexpensive planner for their use. Talk to them about the importance of using the planner daily, and getting into the habit of planning for each day the night before. Explain to them how this will start to free up more time for them to do the things they want to be doing, instead of just doing the things they have to be doing as they become more focused.

In addition to a planner/goal book, have the children create a journal as well, writing down brief entries into a personal journal on a daily basis of things that interest or perplex them is a great way to get them started with being responsible, planning for their future, and allowing them time for natural, real world problem solving!

5. USE YOUR IMAGINATION

Go online or to your library and search for wonderful places around the globe that you would love to visit sometime in your life. Have the kids look through books or at websites. Take notice as to what types of places intrigue them the most and talk about those places. Ask them what they would have to do in order to get to visit these wonderful places. Have them search how much it would cost to fly there if you were to leave today.

What could they do to raise enough money for a trip like that? What other expenses may they encounter planning for a trip to that location? If it's something they really want to do, have them list it in their journal as one of their goals and then start to list all the things they need to do in order to reach that goal.

6. BREAK OUT THE SEASONS

Sharpen your children's sense and general memory by playing memory games/puzzles. Play silly and fun games like "Identify that smell" or "Name that object" where children are paired off in teams and try to identify blindfolded certain odors or identify what object they are touching without being able to see it. Not only is it fun but it will also help enhance the brain performance of its participants, thereby increasing creativity and problem solving abilities, two critical ingredients in becoming an entrepreneur!

7. DON'T BE SHY

I know that there are lots of old fashioned parents out there that think that the household finances should be top secret and not o be discussed with children. When it comes to bill time or any time money needs to be discussed, don't be shy. Share with children the expenses and income you manage each month and each year. Show them the bills you pay, how much they are, and when they are due. Explain to them how you make your payments on these bills. If you write cheques to pay them, then have them help you with that. If you pay some of your bills online, have them help with that too. Don't, be shy, show them how you balance your chequebook and keep track of your finances.

If you are not sure how yourself, research it online or at the library and learn it with your children. You would be surprised as to how much kids are interested in learning how to pay bills, balance a bank account, or even create a budget. It increases their interest in math by giving them purpose for learning the subject!

8. TRY SOMETHING DIFFERENT

Have a "what I want to be when I grow up" get-together

with your child and their friends; where everyone comes to the get-together as what they want to be when they grow up. Children play the role and parents encourage them by catering for the children's needs.

You can give prizes to the kids for acting their parts and encourage the role-playing. This will help them see themselves now as they could potentially become in the future, bringing the feelings of success of what it would feel like. By the parents catering for the "grown-ups" needs, the kids get the idea of what respectful/professional treatment would seem like when they actually reach their goals.

HANDS-ON KID ENTREPRENUERS

Many children across the world are venturing into entrepreneurship and making waves for themselves.

Please Leave a 1-click Review!

Thank you for reading this book and engaging in the next step to establishing kids with financial management. I hope this book helped you in the same way it has helped many others.

I would really appreciate if you could take 60 seconds to write a short review for this book on Amazon, even if it's just a few sentences! Your help in spreading the word is greatly appreciated. Reviews from readers like you make a huge difference in helping new readers find helpful books like this one. I joyfully read every single review.

Just click on the link below and you will be taken straight to the review page on Amazon. Thank you!

<u>Review Book Here</u>

CONCLUSION

The point I have emphasised throughout this book is that young children can learn about money from as early an age as three.

Having a healthy attitude towards money is important to help your kid grow with skills that lots of schools are not going to give them. They are going to need them desperately the minute they leave home. If you think they are too young to know about money, remember that one day they will have to pay for their expenses.

THE BOOK

This author observes how kids today are bombarded with advertising, and keep up peer pressure. She sees money management and financial skills as a must subject matter for parents to continually cover with their kids throughout their childhood and teen years. The tips to do just this are presented in this book in clear readable way for all to understand, follow and apply.

If your kids become financially responsible at an early age, chances are much greater they will continue throughout their lifetime. This is an aim this book can help you fulfil.

OTHER BOOKS YOU'LL LOVE!

CLICK ON THE BOOKS

Link to Book

272 | OTHER BOOKS YOU'LL LOVE!

Link to Book

Link to Book

OTHER BOOKS YOU'LL LOVE! | 273

Link to Book

Link to Book

274 | OTHER BOOKS YOU'LL LOVE!

Link to Book

Link to Book

OTHER BOOKS YOU'LL LOVE! | 275

Link to Book

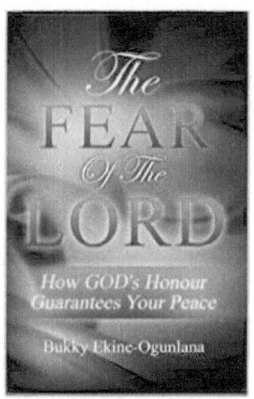

Link to Book

276 | OTHER BOOKS YOU'LL LOVE!

[Link to Book](#)

REFERENCES

1. https://www.fnbwford.com/pdf/Talk%20to%20your%20kids%20about%20money.pdf
2. https://money.usnews.com/money/personal-finance/family-finance/articles/how-to-help-adult-children-become-financially-independent
3. https://www.ats.edu/uploads/uploads/lancaster-spending-plan-workbook.pdf
4. https://www.foolproofme.org/studentpirgs/images/Student_PIRGs_debt_trap_brochure-print.pdf
5. https://www.daveramsey.com/blog/how-to-teach-kids-about-money
6. https://www.nomoredebts.org/budgeting/budgeting-tips/smart-money-management-ideas-for-kids

7. https://masassets.blob.core.windows.net/cms/files/000/001/092/original/Difficult_Conversations_-_Talking_about_money.pdf
8. https://www.waldorflibrary.org/images/stories/articles/giftofno_mcglauflin.pdf
9. https://www.gogoshopper.com/resources/learning-the-value-of-money-lesson-plans-and-activities.html
10. https://www.practicalmoneyskills.com/assets/pdfs/lessons/lev9-12/TG_Lesson10.pdf
11. https://www.daveramsey.com/blog/stop-impulse-buys
12. https://www.sec.state.ma.us/sct/sctinv/pdf/Danger_of_Credit_Cards.pdf
13. https://www.researchgate.net/publication/4886768_Pocket_money_and_child_effort_at_school
14. https://www.theatlantic.com/family/archive/2018/12/rich-people-happy-money/577231/

www.ingramcontent.com/pod-product-compliance
Lightning Source LLC
Chambersburg PA
CBHW021141080526
44588CB00008B/161